TAR HEELS

FIVE POINTS IN THE RECORD OF NORTH CAROLINA
in the Great War of 1861-5.

*New Introduction and Material
By Patrick A. Schroeder*

SCHROEDER PUBLICATIONS
2001

NASH BROTHERS
BOOK AND COMMERCIAL PRINTERS
GOLDSBORO, N. C. 1904
REPRINTED WITH A NEW INTRODUCTION
AND ADDITIONAL MATERIAL BY
PATRICK A. SCHROEDER

REPRINT THIRD EDITION

This book is printed on acid-free paper.

Front Cover: The *Tar Heel* made by North Carolina veterans stating their proud claims. It reads: 1861-1865 The Tar Heels roll of Honor North Carolina, with a male population (military age) of 115,000, furnished 127,000 Confederate Soldiers, lost 40,375 of her brave sons, double the loss of any other state, with 5000 to spare. First at Bethel, Foremost at Gettysburg, Furthest at Chickamauga, the Last at Appomattox. "God Bless North Carolina" R. E. Lee. The banner is in the North Carolina Museum of History Collection.

Back Cover: This painting of the gallant and noble James Johnston Pettigrew is in the North Carolina Museum of History Collection.

Cover Design by Maria Dorsett Schroeder

Printed by Sheridan Books
Fredericksburg, Virginia

ISBN-1-889246-15-8 (Hardcover)
ISBN-1-889246-02-6 (Paperback)

Published by
SCHROEDER PUBLICATIONS
12 Camellia Drive
Daleville, VA 24083
paspub@rbnet.com
www.civilwar-books.com

INTRODUCTION

Tar Heels: Five Points in the Record of North Carolina in the Great War of 1861-5 is a book by soldiers who strove to make those points honored in the history of their state and of the nation. The five points refer to North Carolina's proud claims "First at Bethel, farthest to the front at Gettysburg and Chickamauga, and last at Appomattox." Appomattox generates two points--the last volley fired by the Army of Northern Virginia and its last capture of Union artillery.

In 1903, Virginia Judge George L. Christian questioned the veracity of North Carolina's claims. Tarheel veterans felt obligated to research and present a historical account upholding their viewpoint. Each member of the committee had a distinguished war record, and in most cases participated in the engagement they reported on. In the following text, they defend their heartfelt beliefs with an abundance of first-hand accounts, reports, statistics, maps, logic, and corroborating testimony from their Federal foe.

Even today, the role of North Carolinians is largely overlooked. Pettigrew's, Scales', Davis' and Lane's brigades no doubt advanced farther to the left of "the Angle" during Longstreet's July 3, 1863, assault causing confusion for Webb's Federal brigade in "the Angle." In fact, a member of the 42nd New York of Hall's brigade captured the flag of the 22nd North Carolina inside "the Angle."

In Longstreet's July 3 assault, Pickett's Virginians lost an average of 91 men per regiment. Pettigrew's larger units sustained a higher ratio of casualties losing an average of 250 men per regiment. The Gettysburg section may attract the most attention. Yet, North Carolina's participation at Big Bethel, where they suffered the first battle fatality (Henry L. Wyatt of Company A, 1st North Carolina Infantry), and their advance and capture of artillery pieces at Chickamauga are also compelling. "The Last at Appomattox" reveals scarce details about the final battle fought by the Army of Northern Virginia and the prominent role played by General Bryan Grimes and North Carolina soldiers.

Tar Heels: Five Points in the Record of North Carolina in the Great War of 1861-5 is an excellent primary source. However, until now, the book could only be found in rare bookstores, if at all. It is reprinted in its original text, with a corrected index, photographs of key North Carolina commanders and soldiers, and a page citing the inscriptions on the North Carolina monuments at Appomattox.

Patrick A. Schroeder

Esse Quam Videri.

FIVE POINTS

IN THE

Record of North Carolina

IN THE

GREAT WAR OF 1861-5.

REPORT OF THE COMMITTEE

APPOINTED BY THE

North Carolina Literary and Historical
Society--1904.

INDEX

MAPS

PHOTOGRAPHS

PREFACE.

At a meeting of the State Literary and Historical Association held in Raleigh, Nov. 12th, 1903, the following resolution offered by Colonel J. Bryan Grimes was adopted:

Resolved, That the North Carolina Literary and Historical Association ask the following gentlemen, Chief Justice Walter Clark, Chairman, Capt. S. A. Ashe, Senator H. A. London, Hon. A. C. Avery, Hon. W. A. Montgomery, Major E. J. Hale and Capt. W. R. Bond, to act as a Committee to investigate and report upon the accuracy of North Carolina's claim as to the number of troops furnished by this State to the Confederacy, and upon the merits of our claim as to "First at Bethel, Farthest at Gettysburg and Chickamauga, Last at Appomattox."

Upon the resolution Colonel Grimes submitted remarks, in substance, as follows:

"Not many weeks ago at a meeting of the Grand Camp of the Virginia Confederate Veterans, Judge George L. Christian surprised the country by questioning the claims made by North Carolina as to her record in the War for Southern Independence. These assertions of Judge Christian, occupying the position he does, gives his charge such prominence and his article has been given such currency that it should not be allowed to pass unnoticed.

We feel it our duty to our State to refute this disparagement by Judge Christian and it is peculiarly appropriate that this Association should take up this challenge and I wish to offer a resolution to that end.

I do not intend to reflect upon Virginia, and I would not have this resolution construed in that way, but North Carolina has suffered enough in the past by being denied credit for her achievements. Our State has always acted the part of a loving sister to Virginia. In her early Colonial wars it was the North Carolina soldier, who, without reward or hope of reward, assisted in driving the French and Indians from the Virginia border.

In the earliest days of the Revolution the North Carolina

soldier hurried to Great Bridge to stand between the British invader and the heart of Virginia.

In the great Civil War the first soldier sacrificed in defense of Virginia homes was the Carolinian Wyatt and in that long and bloody struggle for every one soldier life that Virginia gave to protect herself, more than two North Carolina soldiers were buried in her soil.

Whenever Virginia has suffered North Carolina has bled. We would disdain to pluck one laurel from Virginia's brow— we love her still—but we say calmly to our beloved sister that she must pause and give us justice. We are worthy of our appropriate motto *Esse quam videri,* and we are ready to prove our claim."

WAR RECORD OF THE COMMITTEE.

WALTER CLARK—*2nd Lieut. and Drill Master 22 N. C. (Pettigrew's) Regt.; 1st Lieut. and Adjutant 35 N. C. (M. W. Ransom's) Regt.; Major 6th N. C. Batt.; Lieutenant-Colonel and Major 70 N. C. Regiment.* Paroled at Johnston's surrender.

E. J. HALE—*Private Co. H., "Bethel" Regt.; 1st Lieut. and Adjutant 56 N. C. Regt.; Capt. and Major A. A. G., Lane's Brigade.* Paroled at Appomattox.

W. A. MONTGOMERY—*Private, Sergeant and 2nd Lieut. Co. F., 12 N. C. Regiment.* Paroled at Appomattox.

W. R. BOND—*Private 12 N. C. Regt.; 2nd Lieut. Co. D., 43 N. C. Regt.; 1st Lieut. and A. D. C. to Gen. Daniel.* Captured at Gettysburg. Prisoner at Johnson's Island.

A. C. AVERY—*1st Lieut. and Capt. Co. E., 6 N. C. Regt.; Capt. and A. A. I. G., D. H. Hill's Corps; Major 17 N. C. Batt.* Captured by Stoneman, April, 1865.

H. A. LONDON—*Private Co. 1, 32 N. C. Regt., and courier to Gen. Grimes.* Paroled at Appomattox.

S. A. ASHE—*Private 18 N. C. Regt.; Capt. and A. A. G., Pender's Brigade; 1st Lieut. C. S. Engineers.* Paroled at Johnston's surrender.

THE REPORT OF THE COMMITTEE.

Upon the monument which this State has erected at the west front of the Capitol in Raleigh in perpetual memory of the fidelity to duty of the sons she sent to the front in 1861-5, is inscribed the legend

"FIRST AT BETHEL
LAST AT APPOMATTOX."

Upon the cover of the five volumes of "North Carolina Regimental Histories 1861-'65" which, compiled by veterans who were actual participants in the events they narrated, have been published and issued by authority of the State, there is stamped the above words with the insertion between the first and last lines of the following:

"FARTHEST TO THE FRONT AT GETTYSBURG AND AT CHICKAMAUGA."

These claims were not made as a matter of boast. They were merely a statement of historical facts, amply supported by the testimony of eye-witnesses and documentary evidence contained in the volumes in question. There was no intention to assert that the soldiers from North Carolina were braver than those from our sister Southern States, but merely that the fortune of war having furnished them the occasion they were *equal to the opportunity*—only this, and nothing more.

"They saw their duty, a dead sure thing
And went for it, then and *thar*."

We also deemed that it was shown beyond question that North Carolina furnished to the Confederacy more troops than any other State. It can not be controverted that, owing to the foresight, practical ability and patriotism of our great War Governor, Zebulon B. Vance, the troops from this State were the best clothed and shod, and the best cared for in the Confederacy.

The above propositions, save the last, having been controverted by Judge Christian of Virginia in a pamphlet issued by authority of the United Confederate Veterans of that State, the undersigned Committee were appointed by the North Carolina Historical and Literary Society to make reply. The committee met 12 May, 1904, being the 40th anniversary of a day which is forever memorable in North Carolina from the valor of her sons at the deadly "Horse-Shoe" at Spottsylvania. With a view of placing our reply upon the testimony of eye-witnesses the work was sub-divided and allotted as follows:

"First at Bethel," Major E. J. Hale.
"Farthest to the front at Gettysburg," Judge W. A. Montgomery and Capt. W. R. Bond.
"Farthest to the front at Chickamauga," Judge A. C. Avery.
"Last at Appomattox," Senator Henry A. London.
"Number of Troops furnished by North Carolina and the number of killed and wounded," Capt. S. A. Ashe.

These articles were ready by 25 August, 1904, another glorious anniversary to North Carolina Veterans, recalling the successful charge of Cooke's, Lane's and MacRae's brigades at Reams Station 25 August, 1864, which might well be styled a "North Carolina Victory." After being carefully reviewed and corrected, these six articles have been unanimously adopted by the Committee as a true and modest statement of the matters therein severally treated, and they are herewith published as part of this report.

BETHEL.

Major Hale, who was at Bethel—and indeed, continually in service throughout the war and saw its close at Appomattox —tells convincingly the story of the first battle of the War. North Carolina can well claim to have been "First at Bethel," for this first victory for our arms was won by her sons. Not that she had the only troops there. Such has never been her claim, but more than two thirds of the soldiers present— over 800 out of the 1200—were hers and without them the battle would not have been fought. The moral prestige of this first success was very great, and this State justly claims credit for her promptness in placing her troops upon Virginia soil and repulsing the first advance of the enemy. The first soldier killed in battle was Henry L. Wyatt of the "Edgecombe Guards," Co. "A," 1st N. C. Volunteers (later designated by a special Act of the General Assembly "The Bethel Regiment") who fell at Bethel 10 June, 1861. There is no claim that he was any braver than hundreds and thousands who fell ere the red curtain of war was rung down, but his death shows that at the *first* onset the men of this State were ready unto death. Neither is it denied that Capt. Marr, of Virginia, was killed a few days before at Warrenton, Virginia, but that was not in battle. Wyatt was the first to fall in open fight, when troops met for the first time in battle array.

GETTYSBURG.

That the soldiers of this State went somewhat farther at Gettysburg than any others in the third day's battle is so succinctly and clearly shown by Judge Montgomery and Capt. W. R. Bond in the articles by them that it is not necessary to recapitulate. The controverted point assigned us was only as to that charge, else we could have referred to the undisputed fact that on the evening of the second day Hoke's Brigade commanded by Col. Isaac E. Avery (who lost his life in the assault), together with Louisianians from Hays' Brigade, climbed Cemetery Heights, being further than any other troops penetrated during the three days. The following inscriptions placed by the Federal Park Commissioners upon tablets locating the position and stating the services of Hoke's brigade on the second day and Pettigrew's on the third day amply vindicate the justice of our claim. (The tablets also record their glorious services upon the other two days which are omitted here).

"Hoke's Brigade.

2 July. Skirmished all day and at 8 P. M. with Hays's brigade charged East Cemetery Hill. Severely enfiladed on the left by artillery and musketry it pushed over the infantry line in front, scaled the Hill, planted its colors on the lunettes and captured several guns. But assailed by fresh forces and having no supports it was soon compelled to relinquish what it had gained and withdrew. Its commander, Col. Isaac E. Avery was mortally wounded leading the charge."

"Pettigrew's Brigade.

July 3. In Longstreet's assault this brigade occupied the right centre of the division and the course of the charge brought it in front of the high stone wall north of the Angle and *80 yards further East*. It advanced very nearly to that wall. A few reached it but were captured. The skeleton regiments retired led by Lieutenants and the brigade by a Major, the only field officer left."

Judge Montgomery and Captain W. R. Bond were both present at Gettysburg and the former has recently revisited the battle-field. Their array of proof as to the North Carolina Troops is further sustained by the map of the battle-field made by the Federal Commissioners, after years of study of the ground and hearing the evidence of participants from both armies and all parts of the country. A copy of that map is published with their articles. Two other maps herein throw further light upon that historic field.

Without trenching on the ground covered by Judge Montgomery and Capt. Bond and merely as testimony of what troops went where the red rain of battle fell heaviest, it may be well to recall the following facts from the official reports: At Gettysburg 2,592 Confederates were killed and 12,707 wounded. Of the killed 770 were from North Carolina, 435 were Georgians, 399 Virginians, 258 Mississippians, 217 South Carolinians and 204 Alabamians. The three brigades that lost most men were Pettigrew's N. C. (190 killed); Davis's Miss. (180 killed) which had in it one N. C. Regiment, and Daniel's N. C. (165 killed). Pickett's entire division had 214 killed. No brigade in Pickett's division lost as many killed and wounded as the 26 North Carolina regiment, whose loss was 86 killed and 502 wounded, the heaviest loss of any regiment, on either side, in any battle during the war. In the first day's fight there were 16 Confederate brigades of which 7 were from North Carolina. In Longstreet's Assault, which has been miscalled by some "Pickett's charge", there were 19 Virginia and 15 North Carolina regiments besides troops from other States.

CHICKAMAUGA.

Judge A. C. Avery, who was a participant in the battle

of Chickamauga, has lately revisited that battlefield with a view to writing his very graphic article which will have a peculiar interest because the deeds of North Carolina soldiers in the Army of the West are less widely known among us than the daring of the veterans in the Army of Northern Virginia in which the greater part of troops from this State served. Judge Avery clearly shows that the 39, 58 and 60 N. C., the one on the first day and the others on the second day, achieved the farthest advance attained by our troops. This conclusion is further sustained by the locations marked on the map by the Federal Commissioners, as having been attained by the different troops. The map of Chickamauga accompanying Judge Avery's article was made under his supervision after revisiting the field. Judge Avery states that while these locations have been marked on the ground by tablets erected not only by the Northern States, but by South Carolina, Georgia, Alabama, Tennessee, Missouri and other Southern States, the highest point, that reached by the North Carolinians, is marked only by a wooden board nailed to a telegraph pole! Moved by this pathetic statement, the committee adopted the Resolution which will be found below.

APPOMATTOX.

Senator Henry A. London, who carried the last order at Appomattox, tells tersely and clearly what he saw and heard and is fully sustained by the statements which he quotes of Major-General Bryan Grimes and Brigadier General Cox who were in command of the troops who fired the last volley. Two other members of the Committee, Major Hale and Judge Montgomery, were also at Appomattox. The positions held by the troops under Major Gen. Grimes, who were in the front of the army and by whom necessarily the last volley was fired, (the other part of the army under Longstreet, which faced Grant, in our rear, was not engaged) is shown on the map accompanying London's article herein. The ground was visited 1 Oct., 1904, by a special committee consisting of Hon. H. A. London, Judge W. A. Montgomery, Capt. W. T. Jenkins and Mayor A. M. Powell, veterans of that field and they were accompanied by W. J. Peele, Esq., Chairman of the State Historical Commission to whose patriotism and intelligent aid your Committee and the Confederate Veterans are greatly indebted. The localities were identified and measurements taken from which the excellent map of Appomattox accompanying their report was prepared for which thanks are due to Prof. W. C. Riddick of the A. & M. College.

The article of Hon. E. J. Holt who commanded the 75 N. C. Regiment (7th Cav.) at Appomattox shows that the cavalry made their last charge very nearly as late as the time Cox's infantry fired the last volley and that shortly before a battery of 4 guns and 50 prisoners were captured by Roberts' N. C. Cavalry brigade (to which that regiment belonged) being the very last capture made by that immortal army which had made so many.

NUMBER OF TROOPS AND LOSSES.

Capt. S. A. Ashe sustains, from a careful examination and collection of the records, that North Carolina furnished by much the largest number of troops of any State to the Confederacy. Lieut.-General Stephen D. Lee (Commander in Chief of the United Confederate Veterans) in a very recent address at Asheville stated that "North Carolina furnished 22,942 more troops than any other State." If this were not so, it redounds even more to the fame of the State, for North Carolina lost according to the official returns—as compiled in Colonel Fox's "Regimental Losses"—over 41,000 killed and wounded and died of disease according to "U. S. Official Records" while the Confederate Hand-book gives: *Virginia, 5,328* killed, 2,519 died of wounds, 6,947 died of disease, total 14,-794. *North Carolina, 14,452* killed, 5,151 died of wounds, 20,602 died of disease, total 40,305 a number considerably in excess of that sustained by any other Southern State.

Owing to her innate modesty North Carolina, notwithstanding she furnished nearly one-fifth of the Troops of the Confederacy, fell far short of one-fifth of the 608 generals appointed during those four memorable years. Instead of 120, our proportion according to troops furnished, we had 2 Lieut. Generals, 7 Major Generals and 26 Brigadiers, a total of 35 generals, of whom nine were killed in battle and several others were invalided by reason of wounds. Yet we were not lacking in material. Upon the death of Major General Pender, a superb soldier, General Lee publicly deplored that "General Pender had never received his proper rank," and in the opinion of the whole army, the hero of Plymouth, that splendid soldier, Robert F. Hoke, who was a Major General at 26, merited the command of an Army Corps; and there were many others who deserved the rank of Major General and Brigadier General which was given to men, certainly not their superiors, from states with a smaller proportion of troops to general officers.

But it is not to her generals and lesser officers, capable and faithful as they were, that North Carolina should turn with her greatest pride. With tacit recognition of this truth, the State has appropriately crowned the Monument raised to her gallant dead with the statute of

A PRIVATE SOLDIER,

with belted cartridge box, and his faithful musket in hand, *on guard,* scanning the horizon, as in life, with ceaseless watching for the foe. General A. P. Hill, of Virginia, when asked what troops he preferred to command, replied "Unquestionably North Carolinians—not that they are braver where all are brave, but brave as the bravest, they are the most obedient to command." It was this marked trait which gave the troops from this State their pre-eminence. It was the same quality which gave to the Roman soldier his fame and to Rome the empire of the world. History shows no soldier since who more nearly resembles the legionaries of Cæsar than the North Carolina Confederate private. He displayed, together with the same intrepidity, the same uncomplaining endurance of hardship and hunger, the same unquestioning obedience to orders, and wherever the bravest officer dared to lead, there the private soldier from the plains, the valleys and the mountains of North Carolina swept on in his long unbroken lines. They but did as they were told to do and blushed to find it fame. Thus it was that at Gettysburg and at Chickamauga, on the utmost verge of the storm swept sea of battle it was the bodies of North Carolina's slain that marked where highest up the bloody wave had reached and grappled with the hostile shore. Thus it was that, at Bethel, Wyatt fell in the moment of our first victory, and at Appomattox the North

Carolina line, sullenly retiring, fired the last volley over the grave of the Confederacy.

But it is not only for his services during those four memorable and eventful years, that the Confederate soldier should be remembered. His services to his State did not end with the surrender. Other soldiery, demoralized by a long war, have too often returned to their homes to become a standing menace to lawful authority. The disbanded Confederate soldiers at once resumed their places as citizens. Unseduced by the offers and blandishments of those who would have plundered the public, with nerves unshaken by defeat, they took their stand for law and order, and for good government and self government. To them for the past forty years North Carolina, more than to any other source, is indebted for the peace and order which has enabled the State to rebuild its waste places and emerge from the disasters of a long war. In war and in peace, they have stood by their State, faithful alike in' good and evil times, and North Carolina owes no greater debt than to the unshaken fidelity of him whose highest honor is that he was a North Carolina Confederate *Private Soldier.*

One of the most gallant leaders of the splendid soldiery North Carolina sent to the field, Colonel R. T. Bennett of the 14 N. C. Regiment writes:

"We did not make this claim boastingly. The subject is far too near our hearts for vainglory. We thought the recital of these great events in which our people shared so fully and to which they gave free oblations of blood not amiss if perchance the glow of enthusiasm lingered over them. We believed our statements supported by indubitable evidence, chiefest the testimony of the faithful who traversed these fields and marked with their corpses the sad story of the death and sacrifice of our hopes. We disdain to extol our soldiers as excelling in valor the men of Virginia or surpassing in the grandeur of their sacrifice and towardliness these Knights of Chivalry.

The trophies erected to those who sprung to immortal renown from the scene of great actions are not inscribed with poverty of praise—such is not the hymn of the ages.

Our citizens crowding to the front, and carving fame ere the South bled to pallor, conquered the highest elegy ever moulded by the lips of man. Upon these fields where we have staked out our claims in the "death gulch", the Lottery of

Battle favored our soldiers and they writ the story God has in his keeping."

———

Moved by the above recited statement of the neglect to mark on the battle field of Chickamauga the position so proudly and hardly won by North Carolina troops, the following resolution was unanimously adopted by the Committee.

On motion of Walter Clark:

"*Resolved,* That Maj. E. J. Hale, Judge W. A. Montgomery, Judge A. C. Avery and Capt. S. A. Ashe are hereby appointed a Committee who shall prepare a bill and lay it before the next General Assembly with request that it shall adopt the same, which bill' shall provide for the placing of enduring but inexpensive tablets, under the direction of the Federal Park Commissioners at Gettysburg, Sharpsburg and Chicamauga, to preserve the location of the North Carolina troops at the critical moments on those historic battlefields, and also to mark where Wyatt fell in the moment of the first victory at Bethel and the spot where the last Confederate volley rang out the falling cause at Appomattox."

———

As above stated we assert no supremacy in valor for North Carolina troops.   It was their fortune to be to the front at the first victory and at the closing scene, and to ride on the crest at the critical moment of the two great critical battles 'East and West.   On these occasions, as on all others they knew how to do their duty.   Those deeds deserve commemoration, though those who earned this great fame sought only duty's iron crown and but to do the work that lay before them.   With them, as with the sons of this State in every great struggle, the motive has been duty, not display, or as this characteristic of our people has been tersely summed up in the motto of our State, "*Esse quam videri.*"

With these articles and this review and endorsement of their truthfulness by the entire committee, our last duty to our comrades is done.   Generation after generation of men shall pass by and the greatest events shall lose their importance as empires shall fall and the world shall change its masters in never ending succession.   What has been is that which

shall be. But while the world stands man shall not cease
to honor the memory of those who knew how to die for country so long as humanity can furnish men willing and worthy
to follow their example.

WALTER CLARK, *Chairman,*
EDWARD J. HALE,
WALTER A. MONTGOMERY,
WILLIAM R. BOND,
ALFONSO C. AVERY,
HENRY A. LONDON,
SAMUEL A. ASHE,
Committee.

RALEIGH, N. C.
18 October, 1904.

Daniel Harvey Hill, commander of the 1st North Carolina
Infantry at the battle of Big Bethel, Virginia.

"FIRST AT BETHEL."

By MAJ. E. J. HALE.

The legend "First at Bethel" first took form in the inscription on the Confederate Monument at Raleigh. It expressed the prevailing sentiment in North Carolina, and, so far as I am aware, in the Confederacy. An illustration of this sentiment immediately after the battle will be found in the comments of leading Virginia papers.

Said the *Petersburg Express* (see page 104, Vol. 1, N. C. Regiments 1861-65):

"All hail to the brave sons of the Old North State, whom Providence seems to have *thrust forward* in the first pitched battle on Virginia soil in behalf of Southern rights and independence."

Said the *Richmond Examiner,* the leading paper of Virginia and of the Confederacy (Ibid.):

"Honor those to whom honor is due. All our troops appear to have behaved nobly at Bethel, but the honors of the day are clearly due to the splendid regiment of North Carolina, whose charge of bayonets decided it."

1. The First North Carolina Regiment, commanded by Colonel D. H. Hill (later lieutenant-general), was not only the first regiment sent by the government to Yorktown to reach there (May 24th—see pages 80-81, Vol. 1, N. C. Regiments, 1861-65),but it was the first regiment to arrive at Bethel (June 6th) and the only Confederate regiment there until after the close of the battle. (See reports of Col. Magruder and Col. Hill, pages 91-97, Vol. II, Series 1, Official Records of the War.)

2. It constructed the enclosed work, or fortified camp, (Hill's report, page 93, Ibid.), which gave protection to most of the troops engaged, by means of which our losses were rendered nominal (Randolph's report, page 101, Ibid.) and without which the enemy probably could not have been defeated. Col. Hill, in his report (page 95, Ibid.) speaking of the crisis of the battle, said: "Captain Bridgers * * * drove the Zouaves out of the advanced howitzer battery [which had been

abandoned by the troops stationed there, under orders] and re-occupied it. It is impossible to over-estimate this service. It decided the action in our favor." Col. Magruder, in his report, (page 92, Ibid.) described the re-capture of the battery by Captain Bridgers as having been made "at a critical period of the fight." The other critical event in the battle was the assault led by Major Winthrop, General Butler's Aide-de-Camp. He was killed and his troops (1st Vermont and 4th Massachusetts, 600 men) defeated by Companies B, C, G, and H, of the North Carolina regiment. Of this fight Col. Hill said (page 95, Ibid.): "It completely discouraged the enemy, and he made no further effort at assault."

3. In the first hasty report which Col. Magruder sent, from the battlefield, to the Secretary of War, (page 91, Ibid.), he said, referring to the numbers engaged on both sides: "Ours about 1,200 engaged; 1,400 in all." In his second report (Ibid., page 92), he said: "Our force, all told, about one thousand two hundred men." Col. Hill, in his report to Col. Magruder (Ibid., page 97) said: "The Confederates had, in all about one thousand two hundred men in the action." On page 96, he said: "There were not quite eight hundred of my regiment engaged in the fight." On the same page he mentions also the presence of "a detachment of fifteen cadets from the North Carolina Military Institute." The two may be considered as equal to 800. The difference between this number (800) of North Carolinians and the total given by Col. Magruder and Col. Hill (1,200) represents the number of other troops at Bethel; so that North Carolina had twice as many (800) as all the other troops combined (400).

4. Col. Hill's report (page 96, Ibid.) gives the list of casualties at Bethel. They were seven (7) in number (including Wyatt) in his regiment, and three (3) in Randolph's Howitzer Battery. The casualties suffered by North Carolina were therefore as 2½ to 1.

5. Major Hotchkiss, the war historian of Virginia, says (page 140, Volume 111, Confederate Military History): "It is generally admitted that young Wyatt was the first Confederate soldier killed in action in Virginia during the Civil War." As Bethel was the first pitched battle of the war, Wyatt was the first Confederate soldier killed in battle in the

war. Col. Magruder, describing Wyatt's death, said in his report (page 92, Vol. 11, Series 1, Official Records of the War) : "Henry L. Wyatt is the name of this brave soldier and devoted patriot. He was a member of the brave and gallant North Carolina regiment."

The word "first", then, used in connection with the victory at Bethel, the first pitched battle of the war, and descriptive of North Carolina's achievements and losses there, may be said to refer with truth to these facts, viz:

1. Her first Regiment of Volunteers was the first to arrive at Bethel.

2. Her troops were first in the work done there.

3. Her troops were first in numbers there, being as 2 to1.

4. Her losses were first in number there, being as 2½ to 1.

5. It was a member of her regiment there who was the first to fall in battle in the war.

The writer, who was present at the Battle of Bethel, notes that Judge Christian makes another complaint under this head. He complains (page 7 of his pamphlet) that, on page 123 of Volume 1, "North Carolina Regiments, 1861-65," the claim is made "that one of the effects of the fight made by the 'Bethel Regiment' was the 'possibly holding Virginia in the Confederacy' "; and he declares this to be the "unkindest cut of all" at Virginia.

The words "possibly holding Virginia in the Confederacy" occur in the "Conclusion" to the history of "The Bethel Regiment, The First North Carolina Volunteers," and are one of a number of summary deductions from the preceding text. The words complained of were a legitimate deduction from the statements made by Major Jed Hotchkiss, the author of the Virginia Volume (111) of the "Confederate Military History," describing therein the condition of affairs in Virginia at the time, and some of which statements are reproduced in the history of "The Bethel Regiment" on pages 80-81. One of these statements by Major Hotchkiss (page 128, Vol. 111, Confederate Military History) is as follows:

"D. G. Duncan, the special agent of the Confederate Government, from Richmond, reported to Secretary of War L. P. Walker, that intelligent and distinguished men in Richmond 'believe Virginia on the very brink of being carried back, and say no man but President Davis can save her.' " [That was May 7th, Ibid., page 129.]

Another of the statements made by Major Hotchkiss (page 129, Vol. 111, Confederate Military History) is as follows:

"From Richmond, on the 11th, [of May], Rev. Dr. W. N. Pendleton, of Lexington, Va., (afterward Captain of the Rockbridge artillery, and later colonel and brigadier general of artillery), wrote to President Davis: 'As you value our great cause, hasten on to Richmond. Lincoln and Scott are if I mistake not, covering by other demonstrations the great movement upon Richmond. Suppose they should send suddenly up the York river, as they can, an army of 30,000 or more; there are no means at hand to repel them, and if their policy shown in Maryland gets footing here, it will be a severe, if not a fatal blow. Hasten, I pray you, to avert it. The very fact of your presence will almost answer. Hasten, then. I entreat you, don't lose a day.' "

Another statement made by Major Hotchkiss (pages 129-130, Ibid.) is as follows:

"Major Benjamin S. Ewell, in command of the Virginia militia at Williamsburg, wrote on the 11th [of May] to Adjutant-General Garnett that a better disposition to volunteer in the service of the State had been evinced by the citizens of James City, York and Warwick, and he hoped to be able to report within a week five or six companies mustered in and doing camp duty; that in Elizabeth City county, volunteers and militia numbered about 600 men, so that about 1,200 could be raised on the peninsula. He asked for arms and a battery of field pieces for these men, and for cadets to drill them. In a private letter of the same date, Major Ewell informed General Lee that there was a disaffection in the Poquosin island section of York county, from which there had been no volunteers, and it might be well to give him authority to call out the militia of the Sixty-eighth regiment from that section if found necessary."

Another statement of Major Hotchkiss, (page 131, Ibid.) is as follows:

"Brig.-Gen. Benjamin F. Butler, of the Massachusetts militia, was assigned, on the 22nd of May, to the command of the 'department of Virginia', with headquarters at Old

Point Comfort, and nine additional infantry regiments were sent to that place."

Another statement by Major Hotchkiss (page 131, Ibid.) is as follows:

"Major Cary reported to Colonel Ewell at Williamsburg, that this demonstration [by a Federal regiment against Hampton, on May 23rd] indicated the propriety of removing his camp farther from Hampton, where the people had responded indifferently to his call for aid in erecting intrenchments."

These statements, made by Major Hotchkiss, the authorized war historian of Virginia, were accepted as mere historic facts and treated accordingly. In reproducing them from Major Hotchkiss's Virginia history, no reflection, of course, was intended upon the patriotic State of Virginia. The victory at Bethel re-shifted the theatre of war from the Peninsula to the Washington line of approach to Richmond, and nothing more was heard of the disaffection reported by Major Hotchkiss.

If, then, the First North Carolina regiment was the chief factor in gaining this victory, the words "possibly holding Virginia in the Confederacy," applied to its work there, was a legitimate deduction from Major Hotchkiss's history.

E. J. HALE.

FAYETTEVILLE, N. C.,
25 August, 1904.

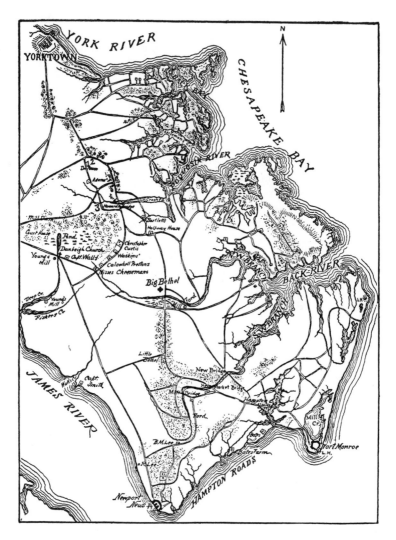

BATTLE OF BETHEL, 10 JUNE, 1861.

"CAROLINA FARTHEST TO THE FRONT AT GETTYSBURG."

By JUDGE W. A. MONTGOMERY.

From the hour when General Lee, riding with General Longstreet at the head of the 1st Corps for the concentration of his army at Cashtown, apparently calm and confident, but really deeply anxious and depressed whether for the unfortunate absence of the Cavalry or because of his need of General Jackson's counsel, heard with amazement the guns of A. P. Hill in conflict with those of the enemy toward Gettysburg, discussion, contention, disputation over almost all of the important parts taken by the different bodies of the troops and the conduct of those in command of them in the battles which immediately followed, have been legacies ever in present enjoyment.

That such has been the case is not a matter for surprise, for, the Confederacy received its death wound at Gettysburg notwithstanding it made afterwards through its armies great and heroic displays of strength on other battle fields, notably, Chickamauga, Wilderness, Spottsylvania and Cold Harbor; and it was almost natural to expect that there would be disparagement of the conduct of some and an undue extolling of that of others in the effort to fix the responsibility of failure.

North Carolinians, continuously, from the moment when the assault under General Longstreet's direction on the Union forces upon Cemetery Ridge was made, have claimed that in that assault the troops from their State went "farthest to the front." There has been controversion, all along, by Virginians of that claim, and at no time, nor by any one, has the denial been so strongly stated as by Judge Christian in "An Official Report of the History Committee of the Grand Camp C. V., Department of Virginia," published under the auspices of that society.

In the pamphlet, too, as might have been anticipated, the honor which North Carolinians think themselves entitled to, the author insists is the rightful due of Virginians won by Pickett's Division. The style of the author is clear and elegant, and the spirit in which he wrote, admirable.

We would approach the subject in a similar temper with no hope, however, of emulating the style and eloquence of the distinguished writer. Nevertheless, upon a review of the matter and after an examination of all accessible information, it is thought that North Carolinians ought not to recede from the position they have all along taken. They are aware that their assertion is valueless without sufficient and competent evidence to support it; and they recognize, also, that not only is the burden of proof upon them, but that they are met *in limine* with the adverse official report of General Longstreet and the opposing writings (subsequent) of Colonel Taylor, General Lee's chief of staff, (Four Years with General Lee) and, General Long, at that time General Lee's Military Secretary, (Memoirs of Robert E. Lee) and Colonel Alexander, Director of Confederate Artillery on that day. (Letter to the Southern Society Papers, Vol. 4.) From all these sources except Col. Alexander's letter it is made to appear that Heth's Division Commanded by Pettigrew, and Lane's and Scales' brigades under Trimble, as a second line, were repulsed and driven from the field in disorder, and that Pickett with his division was left alone to make the charge. Col. Alexander thought that Heth's division went in on Pickett's *right* and too late to accomplish anything.

Colonel Taylor, after reciting that Heth's division faltered and finally retired and mentioning other embarrassments of Pickett's division, continued: "In spite of all this, it (Pickett's division) steadily and gallantly advanced to its allotted task. As the three brigades under Garnett, Armistead and Kemper approached the enemy's lines a most terrific fire of artillery and small arms is concentrated upon them; but they swerved not—there is no faltering; steadily moving forward they rapidly reduce the intervening space and close with their adversaries; leaping the breast-works, they drive back the enemy and plant their standards on the captured guns, amid shouts of victory." General Long in his Book, after relating that Heth's division under Pettigrew had fallen back in disorder and that on that account Scales and Lane were compelled to fall back while Wilcox perceiving that the attack had grown hopeless had failed to advance, said that Pickett's men were left to continue the charge alone. Then he recites the advance of the Virginians, their leaping the breast-works and planting their standards on the captured guns with shouts of victory. And he goes on, "Now was the time that they, (the supporting columns) should have come to the aid of their victorious comrades; but, alas! Heth's division which had behaved with great gallantry two days before, had not been able to face the terrible fire of the Federal lines; whilst the other supports were too remote to afford timely relief. . . . On every side the enemy closed in on Pickett's Brigades concentrating on them the fire of every gun on that part of the line."

Colonel Alexander wrote, "As soon as it was clear that Pickett was "gone up" I ceased firing, saving what little ammunition was left for fear of an advance by the enemy. About this time General Lee came up to our guns alone and remained there half an hour or more speaking to Pickett's men as they came straggling back and encouraging them to form again in the first cover they could find. A little before this Heth's division under Pettigrew had been advanced, also, but I cannot recall the moment or the place where I saw them, but only the impression on my mind as the men passed us that the charge must surely be some misapprehension of orders, as the circumstances at the moment made it utterly impossible that it could accomplish anything and I thought what a pity it was that so many of them were about being sacrificed in vain. It was intended, I believe, that Pettigrew should support Pickett's *right* flank, but the distance that had to be traversed in the charge got such an interval between the two that Pickett's force was spent and his division disintegrated before Pettigrew's got under close fire." And what General Lee said in his official report must also be added. He there said, "Owing to this fact (the lack of artillery support) which was unknown to me when the assault took place the enemy was enabled to throw a strong force of infantry against our left; already wavering under a concentrated fire of artillery from the ridge in front and from Cemetery Hill on the left, it finally gave way, and the right, after penetrating the enemy's lines, entering his advanced works, and capturing some of his artillery, was attacked simultaneously in front and on both flanks and driven back with heavy loss."

If the foregoing accounts of Longstreet's assault are in fact true accounts, then of course, there is nothing in the claim of North Carolinians that they went "farthest at Gettysburg"; but on the contrary they did not maintain their former good reputation for courage and discipline. It is insisted, though, with great respect for the high authority from which they emanated that those accounts are not founded on the facts. It is believed that there is, and has been, evidence at hand to show that those statements were based neither on positive knowledge, nor upon correct information; that the North Carolina troops behaved with the greatest gallantry and that they went "farthest to the front." Before that evidence is introduced, however, analyses of those accounts will clear the matter of many difficulties.

Of course General Lee's official report is of vast importance. It is to be remembered, however, that his position during the battle was at the edge of Spangler's woods from which Pickett's division commenced its advance, a mile from the line of Webb's and Smyth's brigades where the assaulting column struck the Federal forces. The smoke of battle and the distance from the collision prevented him from seeing what was actually going on there. Major Schiebert, an artillery officer of the German Army, then on a visit at General Lee's headquarters, in a letter published in the Southern Historical Papers, Vol. 5, wrote, that he was in the top of a very tall tree watching the battle and that General Lee came to the tree twice and asked him about the movements of the enemy. General Lee had to rely on the reports of his officers, and it is most reasonable to conclude that he based his report upon that of General Longstreet, who was in charge of the movement, re-enforced as that report was by others of one or two of the officers of Pickett's division, particularly that of Col. Peyton in command of Garnett's brigade after that officer had fallen.

In after years General Longstreet, no doubt after careful study of all the facts and after having revisited Gettysburg, altered his views about the North Carolina troops, and in his Book, "From Manassas to Appomattox," published in 1896, corrected his official report. In the report he said: "Major-

General Anderson's division was ordered forward to support and assist the wavering columns of Pettigrew and Trimble. Pickett's troops after delivering fire advanced to the charge, and entered the enemy's lines, capturing some of his batteries and gained his works, about the same moment, the troops that had before hesitated, broke their ranks and fell back in great disorder. . . . This gave the enemy time to throw his entire force upon Pickett with a strong prospect of being able to break up his lines or destroy him before Anderson's division could reach him, which would in its turn have greatly exposed Anderson. He was, therefore, ordered to halt. In a few moments the enemy marching against both flanks and the front of Pickett's division overpowered it and drove it back, capturing about half of it, who were not killed or wounded." This is what he afterwards wrote in his book: "The enemy's right overreached my left and gave serious trouble. Brockenbroughs brigade went down and Davis' in impetuous charge. The general order required further assistance from the 3rd Corps if needed, but no support appeared. General Lee and the corps commanders were there but failed to order help. Col. Latrobe was sent to General Trimble to have his men fill the line of the broken brigades, and bravely they repaired the damage. Trimble mended the battle of the left in handsome style, but on the right the massing of the enemy grew stronger and stronger. Brigadier-General Garnett was killed, Kemper and Trimble were desperately wounded; Gens. Hancock and Gibbon were wounded, General Lane succeeded Trimble, and with Pettigrew held the battle of the left in steady ranks."

Of course, it is not to be thought that Colonel Taylor or General Long could make any statement about the Assault except upon information, deemed by him, reliable. They were not present on the firing line; and it was impossible therefore for them to have seen what was actually going on there. Major Jones, who commanded Pettigrew's brigade after Colonel Marshall was killed, wrote a few days after the battle, "The smoke was dense, and at times I could scarcely distinguish my own men from Pickett's, and to say that any one a mile off could do so is utterly absurd." Their accounts of the nature of the Artillery fire upon Pickett's division show that they wrote without actual knowledge of the

Confederate Lines ▰▰▰▰▰▰▰▰▰▰▰

FIELD OF LONGSTREET'S

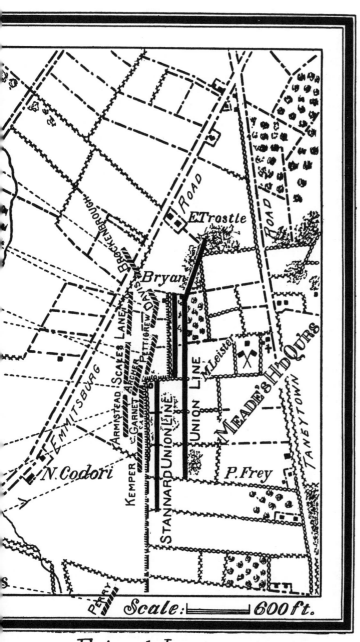

Scale: 600 ft.

Federal Lines ━━━━

GETTYSBURG, JULY 3, 1863.

matter. Colonel Peyton said in his official report, "Up to this time (when within one hundred yards of the rock fence) we had suffered but little from the enemy's batteries which had been apparently much crippled previous to our advance with the exception of one on the mountain about one mile to our right which enfiladed nearly our entire line with powerful effect, sometimes as many as ten men being killed or wounded by the bursting of a single shell." General Hunt who had charge of the Federal artillery on that day in an article published in the January, 1887, Number of the Century Magazine, "I had counted on an artillery crossfire that would stop it (Pickett's division) before it reached our line, but, except a few shots here and there, Hazard's batteries were silent until the enemy came within canister range. They had, unfortunately, exhausted their long-range projectiles during the cannonade, under the orders of the corps-commander, and it was too late to replace them. Had my instructions been followed here, as they were by McGilvery, I do not believe that Pickett's division would have reached our lines. We lost not only the fire of one third of our guns, but the resulting cross-fire, which would have doubled its value."

Colonel Alexander took position on the right and in rear of Pickett's advance. No comment is necessary in connection with his account of the Assault as the part taken by Heth's division further than to say that that division formed on the left of Pickett's, and was never expected to form on Pickett's right; that the troops which Colonel Alexander saw on the right were Wilcox's brigade going into the battle and in support of Pickett, and that Virginians would not be willing to accept the statement that Heth's division *went to close work* with the enemy after Pickett's men had "gone up".

Before reciting the evidence going to show that North Carolinians went farthest to the front at Gettysburg and taking up the discussion of that matter, it is necessary to describe the assailed portion of the Union Line on Cemetery Ridge and to locate and identify the troops which defended the position. The Ridge extends from the Cemetery, south, toward Round Top, two miles away, and along its upper western slope there ran a stone fence. The course of this fence was not an unbroken straight north and south line. For several hundred yards from its southern terminus it ran due north, then turned due east (the space enclosed being called the "Angle") 80 yards and then turned again due north for several hundred yards to the Bryan barn; that is, that part of the rock wall in front of the right of the column of attack stood forward about 80 yards while that part of the wall in front of the left of the column of attack receded inwardly, giving to the enemy's line of defence an *echelon* formation. The Confederate line when it reached the near proximity of that wall exactly equalled its entire length. Posted behind the east side of the rock wall were the troops of the 2nd Corps. (Hancock's).

From the vertex of the "Angle" to the southward along the wall was the 2nd division commanded by Gibbon, with Webb's brigade on the right then Hall's then Harrow's. Along the receding wall from the point where it turned due north was the 2nd brigade of the 3rd division, and then to the North along the wall the 3rd brigade of that division. The 2nd brigade was commanded by Col. Smyth and the 3rd by Colonel Bull, Willard having been killed the day before, and Colonel Sherrell in the present action. Webb's right regiment, the 71st Penn. Volunteers, facing to the west (from which course came the Confederate advance) had its right resting upon the vertex of the "Angle". On the left of the 71st Penn. was the 69th Penn. Volunteers. The objective point in the Federal line, i. e., the point to which the centre of the column of attack, the left of Pickett's and the right of Heth's division, (the latter commanded by Pettigrew) was directed was a cluster of chestnut oak trees that stood inside the union line a little to the rear and left of the 69th Penn. Volunteers. Pickett's division assaulted the three brigades of Gibbon's division, and General Armistead after Pickett's men had reached the wall, with a hundred or more Virginians broke through, and over, the wall in front of Webb and reached a point 33 yards beyond, where he fell mortally wounded, and his followers killed or driven out. General Webb in his official report stated that only a part of the 71st Penn. was driven from the wall and that the 69th Penn. and a part of the 71st Penn. held their positions at the wall. General Gibbon said that the whole front line of Webb was driven back. Numerous North Carolinians of Pettigrew's and Scales' and Lane's brigades and some of Archer's Tennesseans have since the battle claimed that they entered the salient also. But this writer has found no such statement embodied in any of the official reports. The right of Heth's division was at and a little to the south of the vertex of the "Angle". The three North Carolina brigades, Pettigrew's commanded by Colonel Marshall until he was killed and then by Major Jones, Lane's and Scales' assaulted Smyth's brigade along its entire front and a part of Willard's posted behind the receding wall 80 yards to the east of the wall behind which Webb with his brigade and the other brigades of Gibbon's division were posted. For the purposes of this article it makes no difference whether Pettigrew's Brigade of the first line, or Scale's, or Lane's of the second line, in succession or commingled in our line, made the assault on Smyth's brigade. And to digress slightly, it may be as well to add that there was a confusion and commingling of the various commands at and around the vertex in front of Webb. Captain Owen, of Garnett's brigade, in an article in the *Philadelphia Weekly Times* (1881), wrote: "A hundred yards from the stone wall the flanking party on the right coming down on a heavy run, halted suddenly within fifty yards and poured a deadly storm of musket balls into Pickett's men, double-quicking across their front, and under this terrible cross-fire the men reeled and staggered between falling comrades and the right came pressing down upon the centre, crowding the companies into confusion. We all knew the purpose was to carry the heights in front, and the mingled mass, from fifteen to thirty deep rushed toward the stone wall. . . ." The same condition prevailed within the Angle amongst the Federal troops. Gen. Hancock in his official report, after relating that reinforcements had been brought to Webb, said, "The situation now was very peculiar. The men of all the brigades had in some measure lost their regimental organization, but individually they were firm. In regular formation our line would have stood four ranks deep." But to return to the main subject: It is insisted that troops of the brigades of Pettigrew, Lane and Scales, whether in successive lines of battle or commingled in one is immaterial, did advance upon Smyth's brigade behind the receding wall beyond the line held by Webb and before Webb gave way. If they did so advance, then, the presence on the right flank and rear of Webb's first line

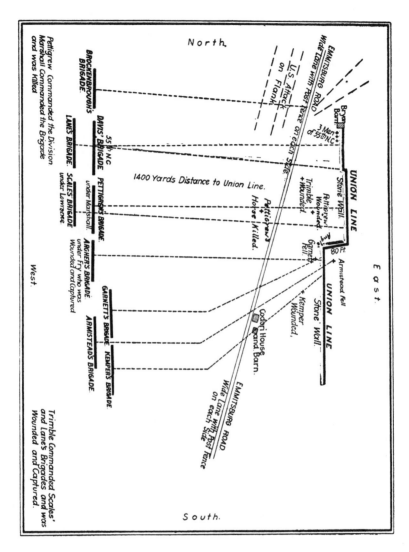

THE FIELD OF GETTYSBURG.

The first positions of the Confederate brigades are shown on the left and then two subsequent intermediate positions, while the final position attained is marked: by the thin line in front of the stone wall and within Gibbon's line on the south of it.

Webb's position in the angle is marked W. Hall's and Harrow's brigades continued the Federal line toward Stannard's brigade.

must have had as great an effect in breaking Webb's line, and forcing it back as the attack in front; and if the North Carolinians continued the advance upon Smyth behind the receding wall further to the east than the point where General Armistead fell, then, not technically, but truly, North Carolinians have made good their claim that their troops "went farthest at Gettysburg." Gen. Armistead was killed thirty three yards to the east of, and in rear of Webb's front line. Now what is the evidence to show that the North Carolinians fought at the left of the vertex of the Angle, that they advanced upon Smyth's brigade behind the receding wall before Webb gave way, and that they went farther toward the receding wall than thirty three yards (General Armistead having been killed thirty three yards to the east of Webb's projecting line) from an imaginary extension of the rock wall in Webb's front toward the north? Colonel Shepard who commanded Archer's brigade, the right brigade of Heth's division, in his official report said, that before the advance was half made his brigade and that of Garnett's the left of Pickett's division, were in touch, and that afterwards when the line reached the rock wall the line seemed to have melted away until there was little of it left, and that four of his regimental flags were captured at the works. That account placed Archer's brigade in front of Webb. Next to Archer on his left was Pettigrew's brigade reinforced by Lane and Scales.

Major Jones of the 26th North Carolina regiment then in command of Pettigrew's brigade, in his official report, stated that, "The brigade dashed on and many *had reached the wall* (italics the writer's) when we received a deadly volley from the left. Major Jones did not have reference to the projecting wall in front of Webb but to the receding wall in front of Smyth. In a letter written by him within the same month of the battle to the father of Colonel Burgwyn (Col. Burgwyn having been killed in the first day's battle) and published early in 1864 in the *Fayetteville Observer,* he wrote, that the color-bearer of his regiment was shot down while attempting to plant the flag on the wall. "I know (he further wrote) we went as far as he (Pickett) did, and I can safely assert some distance beyond, owing to the shape of the enemy's works, which ran backward in my front in the form of a curve. and which compelled us to go beyond where Pickett's men were already at their works in order to reach them ourselves."

Col. Lowrence in command of Scales' Brigade, (General Scales having been wounded in the first day's battle) who went in just where Pettigrew's brigade did, said in his official report that he went forward until the right of the brigade touched the enemy's line of breast-works, as they marched in a rather oblique line. He further said "The two brigades (now reduced to mere squads not numbering in all 800 guns) were the only line to be seen on that vast field, and no support in view." General Lane in his official report said, "The men reserved their fire in accordance with orders, until within good range of the enemy, and then opened with telling effect, repeatedly driving the cannoneers from their pieces, completely silencing the guns in our immediate front, and breaking the line of infantry which was formed on the crest of the hill. We advanced to within a few yards of the stone wall exposed all the while to a heavy raking artillery fire from the right."

In an article published in Vol. 5 of North Carolina Regiments 1861-1865 and written by Major W. M. Robbins, Major of the 4th Alabama Regiment and one of the Gettysburg Battle Field Commissioners since March, 1894, it is said, "And while Armistead and his heroic followers were over in the Angle where were Pettigrew's thin but gallant battalions? They were making a desperate effort to storm the high stone wall 80 yards east of the Angle and were being mowed down like grain before the reaper by the double line of infantry behind that wall. A few men reached it, but finding it too high to leap over could do nothing but surrender. . . I have also stated whither and how far the faithful veterans of Trimble and Pettigrew advanced, which was near the high stone wall before mentioned 80 yards farther east than the Angle and to the left and northward of the spot where the noble Armistead fell. Does any one doubt the accuracy of that statement? If so, I must suggest the undisputed fact that the best proof where a line of soldiers went to is where they left their dead; and where that was in this case is established beyond question by multitudes of disinterested witnesses."

There is strong confirmatory evidence from the Union side of that which we have introduced above.

Colonel Bachelder, one of the first of the Gettysburg Battle-field Commission, and who was thoroughly acquainted with the topography, and the movements of the troops as well, wrote, "The left of the column continued to move on towards the second wall, threatening the right and rear of Gibbons' division which held the advanced line.   General Webb, whose brigade was on the right (in the projection), had hurried back to bring up his right reserve regiment from the second line.   But before this could be accomplished the first line broke under the tremendous pressure which threatened its *front and flank* (italics the writer's), and fell back upon the reserve."

Colonel Smyth who was in command of the second brigade behind the receding wall said in his official report: "My men were directed to reserve their fire until the foe was within 50 yards, when so effective and incessant was the fire from my line that the advancing enemy was staggered, thrown into con-fusion, and finally fled from the field."   And Colonel Swal-low, in the Southern Bivouac for February, 1886, wrote that while he "lay wounded with General Smyth at Gettysburg, that officer told him that Pettigrew's brigade all along his front were within thirty or forty feet of his line and fought with a fury and determination that he had never seen equal-led."

From the above evidence it is submitted without further comment that the claim of North Carolinians that their troops went "farthest to the front at Gettysburg" is well sustained.

Our people, however, do not wish in making their claim to be understood as intending to depreciate the achievements of others on that memorable field.   That would be both un-just and selfish.

Indeed, if it were needed to, here, set down in print an account of the heroism of Pickett's men and the grandeur of their charge on that fateful day, words however eloquent, would be inadequate to express their meed of praise.   No nobler people ever inhabited any spot of our globe than the Virginians of 1861-65 ; no people in the annals of all history, not even the Dutch under the influence of their great William in the terrible Spanish Invasion, ever bore themselves more majestically, more courageously and more unselfishly than did the Virginians under their great Robert E. Lee in the

four years of the war between the States.   And were not the
Confederate soldiers from that State of the same flesh and
blood of its citizenship and children of the great Mother Com-
monwealth ?   And what could be expected of them but that
they would follow their great leader in the path of duty, even
though it led to and through the Union line of battle on Cemetery Ridge ?

WALTER A. MONTGOMERY.

RALEIGH, N. C.,
    25 Aug., 1904.

General James Johnston Pettigrew (left) had three horses
shot out from under him and was wounded in the hand
while leading Heth's division in the July 3, 1863,
assault at Gettysburg.   Pettigrew was mortally wounded
July 14, 1863, at Falling Waters, Maryland, and died
three days later.   After the wounding of General Isaac
Ridgeway Trimble, General James Henry Lane (right) led
the second line attack July 3, 1863, behind Pettigrew.

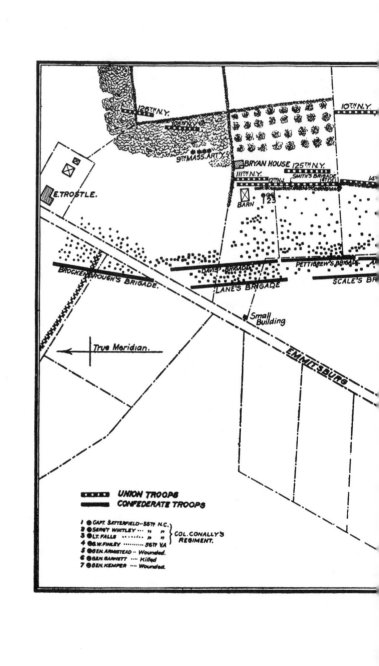

125TH N.Y.

10TH N.Y.

9TH MASS. ART Y.

BRYAN HOUSE 125TH N.Y.

11TH N.Y.

SMITH'S BRIGADE.

E. TROSTLE.

BARN

BROCKENBROUGH'S BRIGADE.

LANE'S BRIGADE

PETTIGREW'S BRIGADE.

LANE'S BRIGADE.

SCALE'S BR

Small Building

True Meridian.

EMMITSBURG

UNION TROOPS

CONFEDERATE TROOPS

1 ● CAPT. SATTERFIELD--55TH N.C.
2 ● SERG'T WHITLEY --- ,,   ,,
3 ● LT. FALLS .... ,,   ,, } COL. CONALLY'S REGIMENT.
4 ● G. W. FINLEY .... 56TH VA
5 ● GEN. ARMISTEAD -- Wounded.
6 ● GEN. GARNETT --- Killed
7 ● GEN. KEMPER --- Wounded.

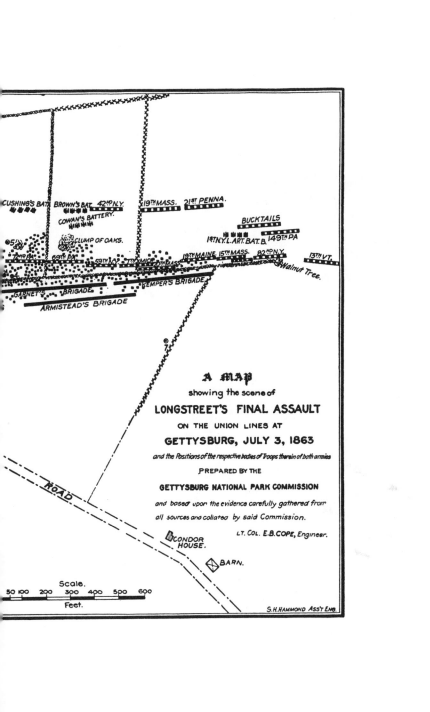

CUSHING'S BAT. BROWN'S BAT. 42ND N.Y. 19TH MASS. 21ST PENNA.

COWAN'S BATTERY.

BUCKTAILS

CLUMP OF OAKS.

1ST N.Y. L. ART. BAT. B. 149TH PA

⦿5TH

72ND PA. 69TH PA. 59TH N.Y. 7TH MICH 20TH MASS. 19TH MAINE 15TH MASS. 82ND N.Y. 13TH VT.

Walnut Tree.

GARNET'S BRIGADE.

KEMPER'S BRIGADE.

ARMISTEAD'S BRIGADE

7.

A MAP

showing the scene of

LONGSTREET'S FINAL ASSAULT

ON THE UNION LINES AT

GETTYSBURG, JULY 3, 1863

and the Positions of the respective bodies of Troops therein of both armies

PREPARED BY THE

GETTYSBURG NATIONAL PARK COMMISSION

and based upon the evidence carefully gathered from

all sources and collated by said Commission.

LT. COL. E.B.COPE, Engineer.

ROAD.

CONDOR HOUSE.

BARN.

Scale.

50 100 200 300 400 500 600

Feet.

S.H.HAMMOND ASS'T ENG.

Brigadier General Alfred Moore Scales (left) was severely wounded in the first day's fighting at Gettysburg. Colonel William Lowrance (right) commanded Scales's brigade during the July 3, 1863, assault.

The three men of the 55th North Carolina who went the farthest in Pettigrew's charge at Gettysburg, July 3, 1863. 1. Captain E. Fletcher Satterfield, Company H, killed. 2. Second Lieutenant T. D. Falls, Company C. 3. Sergeant J. Augustus Whitley, Company E.

LONGSTREET'S ASSAULT AT GETTYSBURG.

By LIEUT. W. R. BOND, A. D. C. to GEN. DANIEL.

The distinguished author of "New York at Gettysburg" says, "Longstreet's assault on the third day had some slight resemblance of success when Armistead and his men crossed the wall—just enough to divert attention from the utter hopelessness of the attempt and relieve the affair from the odium of an inexcusable error. But the slight success of the Confederates would not have been possible, but for the mistake of placing a battery on the front line at the angle. It was through this and at no other place that an entrance was made. Had there been a strong force of infantry on that portion of the line, not a Confederate would have crossed the wall. The storm of bullets would have beaten them back there the same as at every other point of the line. The grand cannonade was a dramatic incident that has unduly magnified the operations of the third day. It was a piece of noisy Chinese warfare that accomplished nothing."

Gen. Meade who characterized the assault as a "mad" and reckless movement was censured in certain quarters for not having made a return attack after the repulse, and his Chief of Artillery Gen. Hunt, though he had no special liking for him, came to his defence by saying "an advance of twenty thousand men from Cemetery Ridge in the face of one hundred and forty guns there in position would have been stark madness."

The strength of the assaulting column was very little if any more than one half of twenty thousand and had Hood's and McLaw's divisions been added it would not have exceeded that number. Gen. Fitz Lee who unjustly holds Gen. Longstreet responsible for the column being as weak as it was says, "why if every man in that assault had been bullet proof and they had arrived unharmed on Cemetery Ridge what could have been accomplished? Not being able to kill them there would have been time for the Federals to have seized, tied and taken them off in wagons before their supports could have reached them."

As to this last extract the words are of course exaggerated, but the idea conveyed in it as in the others is that, in the nature of things the attack could not possibly have succeeded. How different all this from the early accounts by such crude historians as Pollard and Swinton. These writers give the impression that this last attack was repulsed and the battle lost because the North Carolina troops when "weighed in the balance were found wanting." Their unjust and cruel reflections upon the best troops in the best army of the Confederacy, were everywhere, outside of North Carolina, accepted as true. But even the authority of the great St. Paul could not have convinced the Tar Heels that regiments which had suffered as enormously as theirs, could ever have behaved badly. Why, there was one company in the 26 N. C. regiment with three officers and eighty four men. All three of the officers and eighty-three of the men were killed or wounded. There was one in the 11 N. C. regiment with three officers and thirty eight men. Two of the officers were killed and thirty four of the men were struck and the color company of the 38 N. C. had every officer and man hit.

"Truth crushed to the earth will rise again
The eternal years of God are hers."

Less than forty of these eternal years of God had passed ere well informed soldiers everywhere admitted, that the assault was doomed to failure from the start. This admitted, none of the troops engaged can be held responsible for its failure. But now behold "wounded error" shifting his ground and claiming only, that on that crimson field the right division acted the most heroic part. Invoking the assistance of Truth it shall be my purpose to combat this claim.

The report of the Virginia History Committee starts out by saying many pleasant things about N. C. soldiers, but later on it gives extracts from the official reports of officers with the intention of proving that these generous sounding words are not precisely true words and that compliments are not always to be taken literally. One of these extracts is from the report of Col. Lowrance of the 34 N. C. Regiment who though painfully wounded in the first day's battle, commaned Scales' brigade in the assault. The extract tells of how "troops from the front came tearing through our ranks, which caused many of our men to break, but with the remaining few we went forward until the right of the brigade touched the enemy's line of breast works. * * * * * Now all had apparently forsaken us."

Commenting on the report, the address says, "Now the troops in front of Lowrance were Pettigrew's and he says, they gave way a third of a mile before they got to the enemy's works, but be this as it may, he nowhere says that any of his men entered the enemy's works and none of the reports we have seen say that any North Carolina troops did this, which as we have seen is the real point at issue."

Comment No. 1 on this comment is that when Col. Lowrance said that the right of his brigade "touched" the works, of course he meant it reached them. That his troops should have gotten on the other side and occupied them as a captured fort is occupied when a counter attack was to be expected would have been a rather remarkable proceeding even for that field of folly. It used to be laughingly told on that gallant old Confederate General Pillow that on a certain occasion having carried some breast works, he soon lost them in consequence of having placed his men on the side from which the enemy had been driven. This story however was only a soldier's joke. The real case was that this officer led his brigade over the works in pursuit of the enemy, and when the return attack came his men being disorganized by their rush, not only lost the ground they stood upon, but the works they might have held. Had this general (who served in the West) left his brigade at the works and been mortally wounded, while he and a small squad pursued the enemy, he might perhaps have been called a hero or again perhaps he might have been an object of ridicule. No one can tell off hand in what class he would have been placed.

With us consideration of longtiude and latitude had much to do with deciding such matters.

Comment No. 2 on this comment is that it is by no means certain that all the troops in front of Lowrance's were Pettigrew's. This brigade, (Lowrance's) started out in rear Archer's which was on Pettigrew's right but soon Pickett's men were moved to the left, and in crossing the field Lowrance may have drifted to the right, as the close of the assault found a part of them mixed with Armistead's and Garnett's men and part with Archer's.

The Federal Col. Hall gives the names of five flags captured by his brigade. Two of them belonged to Garnett's, two to Armistead's and one to Lowrance's. Carroll's brigade captured one of Armistead's and one of Lowrance's; Smith's two from Archer's one from Lowrance and that of the 52 N. C., the right regiment of the brigade commanded by Col. Marshall. Twenty-eight regimental flags in all were captured. The names of many of them were not reported. Pickett's troops lost thirteen of their fifteen flags. We find in "New York at Gettysburg" this statement: "Private Michael McDonald of this regiment (42 N. Y. Tammany) captured the flag of the 22nd N. C. of Scales' brigade whose troops were commingled with Pickett's at the Angle."

And yet the address says, "We have shown we think conclusively, that the Virginians did penetrate the enemy's line on the 3d of July, '63, in the famous charge at Gettysburg, and that the North Carolinians under Pettigrew and Trimble, did not."

Returning to the comment on Col. Lowrance's report. There is something else that tends to support the contention that the troops which broke through, were not necessarily Pettigrew's, for the late Gen. Dearing (at the time of the battle a Major of artillery and in command of the guns, which moved out with the assaulting column) shortly after this battle told a North Carolina officer, a friend of the writer, that hundreds of Pickett's men went to the rear even before a shot had been fired at them. This is mentioned as a fact and not as a reflection, of the character of a city or state is guaged by its best and not by its worst citizens, and the same rule applies to military organizations. If, when Col. Lowrance says all had apparently forsaken them, he means that at that time the fragments of his brigade and the troops with them at, or near, the salient were the only ones left on the field, he is mistaken, for far over to the left in front of Sherrill's brigade was Lane's North Carolina and there they remained completely dominating the enemy in their front, till they were ordered to retire, and this order was not given till after every other Confederate organization had either surrendered or fallen back. This is the testimony of Generals Trimble and Lane and dozens of subordinate officers and their testimony is strengthened by that of Gen. Hancock who in a dictated dispatch to Gen. Meade said, "I had to break the line to attack the enemy in flank on my right where the enemy was most persistent, after the front attack was repelled." Yes, Col. Lowrance, your N. C. comrades of the old "Light Division," were there. This is the truth, and the shadow of great names will not forever obscure it.

Judge Christian gives an extract from the report of Major John Jones commanding Pettigrew's own brigade, in which he says, "The brigade dashed on and many had reached the wall," etc. To have reached the stone wall on the left of the salient (they must necessarily have advanced much further than did the squad which followed Armistead across the works at the salient. They were nearer the general line of the Federal Army and literally further to the front than any troops of the right division. And when it is remembered that this North Carolina brigade, and its companion brigade, Davis' Mississippi, had fought on the first day, for numbers engaged,.one of the bloodiest, if not the very bloodiest open field battle in the whole Civil War, had they, breasting that storm, only arrived anywhere near the wall in their front, they would have shown an endurance rarely equalled and never surpassed by any troops in Lee's army. Indeed they would have been "the foremost in the display of the qualities of the good soldier," of all the troops upon that field.

The following is an extract from a letter written by a resident of Chicago, Major Charles A. Hall, who has the honor of having served in the 5 New Hampshire, a regiment which fought gallantly at Gettysburg, and is distinguished for having during the war sustained the greatest losses in battle of any infantry or cavalry regiment in the whole Union Army: "There is not a shadow of doubt in my mind but that the sons of North Carolina, Tennessee and Mississippi carved on the tablets of history equal laurels with the sons of Virginia in the great events of that supreme attempt to gain victory at Cemetery Ridge. Pettigrew and Trimble deserve equal honors with Pickett and, if we weigh with judicial exactness, more, for impartial evidence proves that they suffered in a greater degree, and forced their way nearer the lines, where

pitiless fate barred their entrance. The nearest point reached by any troops was Bryan's barn; this is made conclusive
by the evidence on both sides."

Found upon the tunics of the dead soldiers at the Bryan
barn, were buttons bearing the initials of the Old North
State. As to what regiment these men belonged, though I
have an opinion I do not know positively, and do not greatly
care to know. When Major Hall says "the nearest point
reached" he of course means nearest the general line of the
enemy. This gallant officer, Major Hale is mighty good
authority, for not only did he take part in the battle, but for a
number of years was the proprietor of a Cyclorama represent-
ing scenes from this battle and had studied the subject of his
painting thoroughly.

Judge Christian devoted himself in large part to reports of
officers and comments upon them. The most of these reports
are so conflicting that I will not attempt to reconcile them.
Well may have the great Englishman, in whose honor our Cap-
ital City was named, have once said, "human testimony is so
unreliable that no two men can see the same occurrence and
give the same account of it." Should one wish to unravel the
tangled skein of contradictions, he should know that positive
evidence is stronger than negative. All things being equal, the
man who asserts that he knows a certain act was committed because he saw it, is to be believed rather than the one who de-
nies, and gives as his reason that he did not see it. Take for instance Lane's brigade. Generals Lee and Longstreet did not
see these troops and honestly believed that Pickett's men were
the last to leave the field. General Lane says, his people were
the last to leave, and his testimony is supported by that of
General Trimble, and that of the Federal General Hancock.
And Lane's testimony is true, and there should not be the
shade of a shadow of doubt about it.

An apology is made by Judge Christian for the comparatively small losses in killed and wounded, sustained by Pickett's
division, in the statement that it was natural that troops
which fought only one day should not have as many killed as
those who fought two days. To me, though I had never made
much of a study of the influences which affect the morale of
soldiers in and after battle, the statement did not account
for the very great difference in loss, for I believed it was the

exceptional and not the natural thing that there should be such a difference. However I wished to get the opinion of Col. Fox, of Albany, on the point, as I entertained a high opinion of his judgment concerning this and other kindred subjects. In writing I submitted to him the following proposition for his decision. "There are two bodies of troops—A and B—of one thousand each who fight in the same battle and meet with the same loss in killed and wounded. A fights one day and is defeated with a loss of four hundred—forty per cent—B fights, defeats the enemy and loses two hundred and fifty—twenty-five per cent. After an interval of one day B again fights, taking in not seven hundred and fifty, but six hundred and is then defeated with a loss of one hundred and fifty men—twenty-five per cent.—and the following is his answer. "In reply to the proposition submitted by you I would say that a regiment that fought the first and third day of a battle has a more heroic record in respect to its casualties than one which was in action one day only—both regiments having the same strength, and losing the same number. When a regiment that has encountered severe fighting, is called upon to go into action the second or third day the men are subjected to a severe mental strain that renders their service particularly heroic in this respect. Furthermore the per centage of loss will be greater than appears in the morning reports of the first day—because after a hard fight no regiment can carry into action again all of the survivors; no matter whether it is the next day or the day after that, you have evidently noticed that after a severe battle many of the men who had acquitted themselves creditably in the fighting were incapacitated for several days, although they may not have been hit. There are no statistics covering this point and one can only judge of its extent from personal observation. The depletion of the ranks from this cause would vary greatly in different regiments." I knew that after a hard fought battle, there would be stragglers, for instance the day after the battle of Sharpsburg when our army was drawn up expecting an attack, Garnett's Virginia brigade had only one hundred in line, and Hay's Louisiana only ninety, I knew that at Gettysburg none of the slightly wounded though unfit for duty for several days appeared on the casualty list, and I was also aware of another fact, namely, that when the reaction comes on, after the nervous strain of battle, there will be men, as brave as any, but with such a temperament that they will be really sick and unfit for duty for several days. But in the case submitted to Col. Fox I allowed only one hundred and fifty of the seven hundred and fifty or one fifth, to cover the absentees from these three causes. It is possible that the allowance of six hundred for duty was too large, but in making the estimate I had in mind troops that were the equals of the best in the army. In the case of Pickett's troops two thousand eight hundred and sixty-three, were killed, wounded and captured. This number taken from the forty-nine hundred who entered the fight leaves two thousand and thirty-seven. Of this number only eight hundred or forty per cent. reported for duty on the morning of July the fifth. Yes, eighty per cent. to report for duty as in the supposed case may have been too large an estimate.

Now for the comparative numerical losses sustained by certain commands:

Pickett's fifteen Virginia regiments had thirteen hundred and sixty-four killed and wounded or ninety one per regiment. There were two brigades in Pettigrew's division which contained eight regiments and the number of the killed and wounded was two thousand and two, an average of two hundred and fifty to the regiment. Five of these eight regiments were from North Carolina and their loss was thirteen hundred and three or two hundred and sixty to the regiment. Had these N. C. regiments lost in their two days battle an average killed and wounded of only ninety-one, and not two hundred and sixty, even then according to excellent authority and in good reason, their conduct would have been more heroic. In the one case the limit of endurance was reached at an average of ninety-one. In the other at two hundred and sixty. That Truth and Justice should crown the first with fame and the other with shame is preposterous. Indeed not more absurd would it be to claim that a babe in swaddling clothes would have more force and power on a battle-field, than a disciplined soldier.

Whether for the sake of political expediency, or for a less honorable cause, the State of Virginia all through the civil war was more favored by those in authority than any other member of the Confederacy. In promotions, in assignments to light and pleasant duty, in votes of thanks; in the punishment of desertions, and in every conceivable way was this favoritism shown.   The discipline of her troops was less rigid than among other Confederates, and difficult and dangerous work except in the case of Jackson's old division was assigned to others.   This was notably so with the Virginians in Longstreet's corps.   After Jackson's death there were three corps, and one of them was commanded by Gen. Ewell who was in ill health and it was thought he would soon retire from active service.   Virginia politicians, who generally got what they wanted, wished to have Gen. Pickett succeed him; but in a measure to justify his promotion over the heads of generals who had "borne the heat and burden of the day" some slight military success was thought desirable to give him prestige.   So it fell out that on that eventful third of July Generals Lee and Longstreet estimating too highly the destructiveness and the demoralizing effect of long range artillery fire, made a fatal mistake in regard to the morale of the Federal Army.

They doubtless believed that Cemetery Heights would be given up without a struggle.   Confiding in this belief Pickett's troops and a part of Hill's Corps were selected with the expectation that they would gain much glory at small cost. That one half the column should have been composed of Pickett's Virginians and the other half of the worst cut up troops in the army can be accounted for by no other reasonable hypothesis, than that it was believed at headquarters that light work lay before them.

Some fifteen or twenty years ago among a series of historical articles which appeared in the "Philadelphia Times" was one by Col. W. W. Wood (at the time of the battle a captain in one of Armistead's regiments) giving an account of the action.   There is good reason for believing that the author was not only a brave officer but a truthful man.   Along with other statements covering disputed points is the following, "The order to go forward was obeyed with alacrity and cheerfulness for we believed the battle was practically over and that we had nothing to do but march unopposed to Cemetery Heights and occupy them."   And again he says, "From the time the charge began up to this moment not a shot had been fired at us, nor had we been able to see because of the density

of the smoke, which hung over the battle field like a pall, that
there was an enemy in front of us. The smoke now lifted
from our front and there right before us, scarcely two hun
dred yards away stood Cemetery Heights in awful grandeur."
Here we have it upon the best authority that Pickett's division was not fired upon till they arrived in "rushing distance."
It is well known that the left of the line was subjected to a
severe artillery fire from almost the very start. Many of its
regiments suffered greatly before the right had lost a man,
by shot or shell, for, however comparatively harmless the
fire of artillery may be to soldiers lying down and hugging
the ground, it is very destructive when they are upon their
feet. In a prize fight the object of each pugilist is to ham-
mer the sore spot—the weak spot. In this assault the left brigade which had done indifferent fighting the first day, now did
none at all. The enemy witnessing their conduct naturally
concluded that the left was the weak spot and acted vigorously
upon that conclusion. Davis' brigade which came next the Virginia brigade which had acted so ingloriously was composed
of the 2 and 42 Mississippi, 55 North Carolina and 11
Mississippi. Three of these regiments had fought the first
day, had gained a victory but with great loss. The 11th Mississippi was on detached duty that day and though it and its
brigade did not go quite as far in the assault as the troops
on their right the loss in killed and wounded for this regiment
was two hundred and two which was over sixty per cent.
Pickett's men had ninety-one killed and wounded to the regiment or about twenty-eight per cent. When all things are
considered, their boody fight on the first. day, their standing
up so long and so manfully this day against so terrific a fire,
both from flank and front (as shown by their losses), it will be
seen that it is possible that "Truth" may proclaim, that
Davis' brigade, though they did not reach the vicinity of the
works, are more deserving of the palm than any other command on the field. For it is not known positively that any
other brigade lost on that day so large a per centage of killed
as they. As it may appear unaccountable that, while one part
of the line was suffering so much from artillery, another part
hardly received a shot, it will be well to mention that the
Federal General Doubleday states in his history that with the
exception of one piece all guns in the immediate front of the

Virginia division were dismounted by our shelling, and also that the Virginia Confederate, Colonel Wood, says the smoke was so dense that he could not see the enemy till he came in two hundred yards of them.

If he could not see them they could not see him and his people. Therefore if the enemy in their front neither had the guns nor could see the Virginians if they had possessed them, it is not so wonderful they did not kill them. It will be admitted that armies are organized for the purpose of inflicting injury upon the enemies of their country and that they and their sub-divisions are to be valued in proportion to their killing capacity. Now it has been estimated that in the civil war Southern soldiers inflicted a loss of about forty per cent. greater than they sustained. Therefore if one should wish to ascertain which of the different organizations of the Army of Northern Virginia gave the best evidence of fidelity and efficiency let him consult the casualty lists, contained in the "*Official Records*" published by the U. S. Government. In these he will find no partizanship, no sickly sentiment and no effort to make the wrong appear the right; but he will find a true story plainly told.

And now in conclusion, I will say that to thoughful and unprejudiced readers the strength of the evidence I have cited to prove the heroic conduct of those men in the left divisions will be, I think, the measure of their surprise and amazement that any of the comrades of these soldiers should have conspired to injure them.

WM. R. BOND.

SCOTLAND NECK, N. C.,
    25 August, 1904.

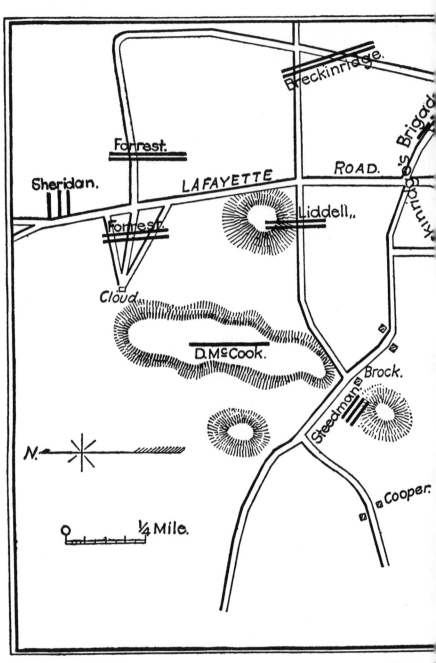

CHIC

Map showing position of the 39th, 58th, and 60th North Caroli

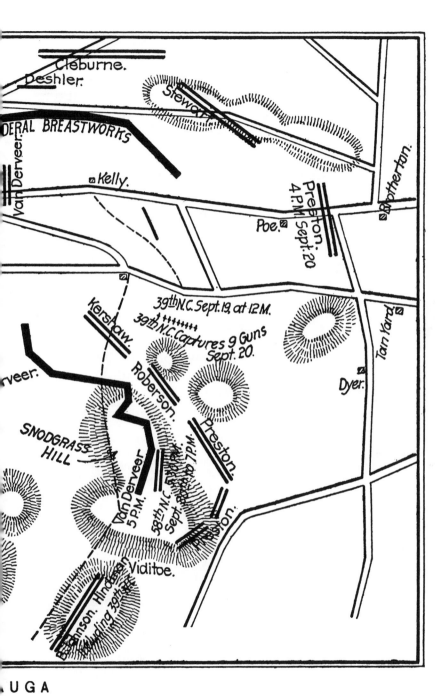

Cleburne.
Deshler.
Stewart.
FEDERAL BREASTWORKS
Van Derveer.
Kelly.
Poe.
Preston.
4 P.M. Sept. 20
Shotterton.
Tan Yard.
39th N.C. Sept. 19, at 12 M.
Kershaw.
39th N.C. Captures 9 Guns
Sept. 20.
Derveer.
Roberson.
Preston.
Dyer.
SNODGRASS
HILL
Van Derveer
5 P.M.
58th N.C. Sept. 20 at 7 P.M.
Preston.
Branson. Hindman. Viditoe.
commanding 39th N.C.

CHICKAMAUGA

Showing the positions at different hours on the 19th and 20th of September, 1863

Colonel David Coleman (right)
of the 39th North Carolina
Infantry commanded McNair's
brigade upon the wounding
of General Evander McNair
at Chickamauga.

Lieutenant Colonel
Edmund Kirby (left) of
the 58th North Carolina
Infantry was killed at
Chickamauga.

Lieutenant Colonel James
M. Ray (right) of the 60th
North Carolina Infantry
was severely wounded at
Chickamauga.

"FARTHEST TO THE FRONT AT CHICKAMAUGA."

By JUDGE A. C. AVERY.

North Carolina sent more soldiers to Virginia than any other of the Confederate States. The State furnished four regiments of infantry and one of cavalry to the army of Tennessee—a smaller representation than that of any State of the Confederacy, except Virginia, which sent only two regiments of infantry, the 63 Virginia of Kelly's Brigade, Preston's Division, and the 54 Virginia of Trigg's Brigade, same Division, and Jeffries' Battery of Preston's Artillery Battalion, though two Virginia .Batteries, Parker's and Taylor's of Col. Alexander's Corps, were sent with Longstreet to Chickamauga, according to the Roster published in the Official Records, Series 1, Vol. XXX, Part II, pages 11 to 17. Four other Regiments of North Carolina Infantry had seen service in Tennessee, two, the 62nd and 64th, were surrendered by Frasier at Cumberland Gap, and two had been transferred to Western North Carolina. Every North Carolina Regiment was assigned to a different division and no two of them fought in the same corps at Chickamauga, except the 39 N. C. of Johnson's Division, McNair's Brigade (commanded by Colonel David Coleman of North Carolina) and the 58 North Carolina of Kelly's Brigade, Preston's Division, both of Buckner's corps. The 60 N. C. Regiment was in Stovall's Brigade, Breckenridge's Division, Hill's corps. The 29 N. C. Regiment fought in Ector's Brigade, Gist's Division, Walker's corps. The 6 North Carolina Cavalry (65 N. C. Regiment) Colonel George N. Folk, participated in the engagement on 18 and 19 Sept., as a part of Davidson's Brigade, Pegram's Division, Forest's Corps.

It was claimed by an adopted son of North Carolina, who was a Federal soldier, fighting in the Brigade, which confronted the 58 and 60 North Carolina, when each of them made itself most conspicuous in attacking Thomas' Corps at Chicamauga, that North Carolina troops reached the farthest point attained by the Confederate State troops. The inexorable logic of the Bible is found, where it assumed, that the unwilling testimony of its enemies was the highest evidence of divine truth. Scarcely less convincing ought to be a tribute from a brave but generous foe to an enemy; whose daring aroused that "stern joy which warriors feel in foemen worthy of their steel." Captain C. A. Cilley, of the 2 Minnesota, was detached as topographical engineer on the staff of Colonel Van Derveer, commanding a brigade of Brannon's (third) Division of Major General Thomas' (Fourteenth) Army Corps and was mentioned in complimentary terms in the reports of both Brigade and Division and Corps Commanders, by Col. Van Derveer as an officer, "whose conduct for efficiency, personal vourage and at every stage of the conflict, was deserving of more than praise," and by General Brannon, for directing two Indiana regiments, in successfully covering the retreat of his division. (See Official Records, Series 1, Vol. XXX, part 1, pp. 423, 431, 433.)

Those who have examined the battlefield of Chickamauga, and followed and studied the movements of troops, must agree, that if Breckenridge's Division of Hill's Corps could have held the Lafayette and Chattanooga road, when Stovall's and Adam's Brigades of that Division crossed on the left and rear of Thomas's corps, before 12 o'clock, on 20 September, 1863, the stronghold of the enemy at Snodgrass Hill would have been turned, placing Hill between Thomas and Rossville and the whole Federal forces in Longstreet's front must have been in full retreat or captured before the middle of the afternoon. Had Walker's Corps or Cheatham's Division moved forward, as a second supporting line, closely after Hill's line, instead of being held in reserve and subsequently sent forward in single lines to be broken in detail, such would have been the inevitable result, as was shown, when the advance in two lines, just before night, forced Thomas to fall back, with a loss of several thousand prisoners. In fact Bragg's plan of battle was to gain the LaFayette road beyond Rosecrans' left (See Boynton's Chickamauga Military Park, pp. 97, 44, 45, 47.)

The 60 North Carolina Regiment, with the 43 and 4 Florida and the 47 Georgia composed Stovall's Brigade (See Series 1, Vol. XXX, Part II, Official Records, at p. 13, Stovall's

Report at p. 231 and Breckenridge's Report at p. 199). This Brigade, General Breckenridge said, flanked the enemy and swept down the Lafayette road, its right resting in that road and Adams' brigade extending the line beyond it. General Breckenridge, describing the situation at the time, said, "Stovall's Brigade gained a point beyond the angle of the enemy's works. Adams had advanced still further, being actually in rear of his entrenchments. * * * * A good supporting line to my division, at this moment would probably have produced decisive results." (See same volume, Report of Stovall, p. 231, and Weaver's report, p. 238.)

Stovall's Brigade drove back two lines, and then changed front. Colonel Ray, commanding the 60 N. C. fell severely wounded, but Captain Weaver held his position, with his right resting on the Lafayette road, until the Florida regiment on his left had been driven back by a flank fire from the line, that had repulsed and killed Helm, and the Forty-Seventh Georgia had been enfiladed and had retired from its right. The 60 North Carolina, with its right on the Lafayette road, in the most advanced location, was the last of Breckenridge's Division to fall back.

Our commissioners appointed under the Act of Congress to mark the positions of N. C. regiments, reported, through Col. C. A. Cilley as Sceretary, 3 November, 1893 (See 5 Clark's Regimental Histories, 169). After a careful examination of maps and comparison of reports, including those of Major-General Brannon of Thomas' Corps and Col. Van Derveer, commanding the Third Brigade of that Division (See Series I, Vol. XXX, Part I, War Records at pp. 429, 430) it was left to Lieutenant General Stewart to designate the furthest point reached by the 60 North Carolina Regiment. General Boynton, of the Park Commission, commanded the 35 Ohio of Van Derveer's Brigade, which met the advance of Stovall at this point, and Captain Cilley, of our Commission, who served on the Brigade staff, were on the ground and aided in the location. Colonel Cilley, for the Commission, reported in part as follows: "The result was that an oaken tablet, suitably inscribed, was put up on the side of the road marking it as a spot, where the Sixtieth North Carolina In-

4

fantry, at noon 20 September, *reached the furthest point attained by Confederate Troops in that famous charge."*

In answer to a recent letter of inquiry the writer received the following reply from Lieutenant-General Stewart, Park Commissioner:

"29 JULY, 1904.

HON. A. C. AVERY, Morganton, N. C.

Dear Sir:—The North Carolina Commission for this Park, visited it a few years since.   I was present when the position of the 60 Regiment N. C. Infantry was marked, at the north end of the Kelly field.   This Regiment formed a part of Stovall's Brigade, Breckenridge's Division, D. H. Hill's Corps: The route pursued by the Brigade on Sunday, 20 Sept., '63 is well established and the extreme point reached by the regiment in its advance, was marked, after very careful examination of the ground and position and is, no doubt, correctly located."

Very truly yours,

ALEX P. STEWART,

Commissioner."

General Boynton (The Chickamauga National Park Commission, pp. 202-204) says, that Stovall had driven John Beatty's line steadily back, Stanly's Brigade had withdrawn from Adam's front, and "the situation was growing desperate," when Van Derveer's Brigade (in which Boynton and Cilley were serving) came upon the scene.   He says, "Stovall and Adams *being unsupported,* were repulsed and forced back around the union left and *the position was saved."*

The foregoing quotations show that, at a crisis, when to hold the position won by the Sixtieth meant victory at noon, the saving of thousands of lives, and the reoccupation of Chattanooga, that Regiment was the last to leave the vantage ground, and would never have receded, had Walker advanced, as a support to Breckenridge, instead of being ordered to stand idle till after the repulse of the first line.   The battle fields of the 19th and 20th are covered with enduring monuments to the Troops of Georgia, Tennessee, Kentucky, and Missouri, though they do not compare with the costly shafts reared by Northern States.   The point attained by the 60

North Carolina Regiment is marked by an inscription on a board, nailed to a telegraph pole, standing beside the Lafayette road. This "wooden tablet" has already done duty as a monument more than ten years.

The 39 North Carolina Regiment, General Bushrod Johnson's Division, was the first infantry of Bragg's Army to cross the Chickamauga. He, with McNair's Brigade, including the 39 North Carolina, crossed at Reed's bridge, and at a ford just above it, and advanced a mile west of Jay's saw-mill (the point from which Cleburn's right moved forward on the afternoon of the next day), and then swept up the Chickamauga for two and one half miles, clearing the way for the other troops to cross. By reference to the reports of Major-General Bushrod Johnson and of Col. David Coleman, of the 39 North Carolina, commanding McNair's Brigade, on 20 September (Official Records, Series 1, Vol. XXX, Part II, pp. 454 and 499), it will appear that being ordered to advance upon the enemy, about 12 M., on 19 September, in support of Grigg's Brigade, Colonel Coleman, in command of the 39 North Carolina, and the 25 Arkansas Regiment (Lieut.-Colonel Huffsteller), finding Grigg's line checked, passed over a portion of it, charged the enemy and drove them three-fourths of a mile across the Chattanooga road, when being unsupported and almost out of communication, they became subject to a cross fire, and were ordered by Col. Coleman to fall back to the main line.

These regiments were the first to cross the Chattanooga road, after the fighting began, and advanced further to the front on the 19th than any other troops went in the attack on Rosecrans' centre before noon of the 20th. Brig.-General Trigg, according to his own report (in the same volume at p. 430) was detained two hours after 12 M., 19 September, and executed several maneuvers under conflicting orders, and then moved forward, until he "came near a corn-field, in which the enemy had a battery, protected by earth-works, near the Chattanooga road." This battery was almost at that road, as appears by the tablets erected by the Park Commissioners. General Buckner made no report of the conduct of Johnson's Division, because it had been previously detached from his corps. General Boynton (at pp. 38 and 39 of his book) confirms Coleman by stating that Johnson's troops were enfiladed by Wilder, when they crossed that road on the 19th.

It is an admitted historical fact, that fifteen Federal guns were captured in the advance, in Dyer's field, where the centre of Rosecrans was broken, about 12 o'clock on 20 September. The map, showing the movements of Johnston's Division (Official Records, Series 1, Vol. XXX, Part II, p. 469) shows the position of six guns captured near the Chattanooga road and nine captured a half mile further on higher ground, in Dyer's field on the 20th. The Federal tablets show the loss of fifteen guns, in the advance of Johnson's Division over Dyer's field.

Col. Coleman, who assumed command, when McNair fell, soon after the forward movement began, (same volume of Official Records last cited, at p. 500) claims, that he captured "ten pieces, eight of which were sent with their remaining horses to the rear." The State Commissioners, with the aid of the Park Commissioners, arrived at the conclusion, that Coleman's regiment captured nine pieces, the troops on his left six pieces. He was a graduate of Annapolis, and after seeing service with the United States Navy at Vera Cruz, in Mexico, resigned his command and read law, gained prominence in his profession and established the character of a chivalrous gentleman. He was not mistaken as to sending eight guns to the rear. With six deserted guns not very far away, he may well have been mistaken in supposing two instead of one was left. Coleman's Brigade and regiment had been sent to Mississippi, when Johnson's report was made. Gregg's Brigade (composed of Tennesseeans and Texans) evidently captured the other six pieces, but the capture of the nine pieces posted on an eminence was the feature of the charge, which broke the enemy's centre and opened the way to assail his natural fortress, Snodgrass Hill, from the South.

Col. Cilley (5 Clark's Regimental Histories, p. 171) says, that, after studying maps and reports on the night before, the North Carolina Commissioners with the Commissioners of the Park, Generals Boynton and Stewart, repaired to the field next day and walked up the long slope of Dyer's Hill, over which ten or twelve Divisions had fought, and a second comparison of all the evidence available, made on the very spot of the conflict, so plainly showed the justice of Colonel Coleman's claim, that our commissioners were directed to "drive down a stake, marked with the regiment's name, the date and fact of the exploit, at the location contended for." The stake is gone. But we may justly claim for Col. Coleman's regiment, that his men have erected a monument more enduring than brass to commemorate their conspicuous courage.

In a letter received from him, after the foregoing was written, Gen. Boynton says, after mentioning other matters,

"In regard to the division of the 15 guns, captured by Sugg's brigade and partly McNair's brigade, commanded by Colonel Coleman, this commission has never received any more definite information upon that subject than is set forth in the reports of General Bushrod Johnson, Colonel Sugg and his adjutant and Colonel Coleman, commanding McNair's brigade. From these reports it is evident, that both these brigades participated in the capture of these 15 guns, one claiming 10 and the other 8. As the difference between these figures and the number captured is only three, neither claim can be much out of the way, and the part taken by each brigade was undoubtedly of the most creditable character."

As will appear later in this article, the 39 N. C. was, as a part of McNair's Brigade, in the charge of Bushrod Johnson and Hindman's Division, which onset first broke the centre of Rosecrans' last line of defence upon the Ridge west of Snodgrass Hill, near the Viditoe House, about four P. M., 20 September.

The 58 North Carolina Regiment was organized in the summer of 1862; but had never participated in a great battle before the afternoon of 20 September, 1863. Preston's Division, on the afternoon of that day, at 4 P. M., was ordered to move from its place in the reserve line at the junction of the Tanyard road with the Lafayette road, cross the bloody Dyer field and relieve Kershaw, who had been vainly assaulting the position of Brannon; on the south side of the protruding knob of Snodgrass Hill, called by the enemy the Horseshoe. In executing the order, Gracie's brigade was on his right, Kelly's in his centre and Triggs on the left. The Fifty-Eighth on the right of Kelly encountered in the charge Van Derveer's brigade, near the intersection of the Horseshoe with the main ridge, which extended south and was defended by Steadman's Division of Granger's Corps. The right of Palmer's 58th extended some distance along the Horseshoe stronghold, while his left was on the ridge. It reached the farthest point in the charge about 5 P. M. A little more than an hour before Bushrod Johnson's Division, including the 39 N. C., in McNair's Brigade, and a part of Hindman's Division had broken the enemy's line, near the Viditoe house, some distance to the left and north. Rosecrans was cut off by this movement and fell back to McFarland's gap with his command, except Thomas's Corps and a part of Granger's, which still held their positions. Such was the situation when the Fifty-Eighth, *on the right of Kelly's brigade, advanced to a point within 15 or 20 steps and its left within 50 yards of Van Derveer's line.* The left maintained its position at this distance during the engagement lasting two hours. The regiment behind its log breastworks in its front was the 35 Ohio commanded by Lieut. Colonel Boynton (now General Boynton of the Commission), (See Boynton's report, Series 1, Vol. XXX, Part 1, p. 436, Official Records.)

Gracie's brigade failed in its assault on the Horseshoe, and in its retreat left the right of the 58 N. C. exposed to an enfilade fire till Robertson's Texans took its place. The right of the 58th was then drawn back, to avoid the enfilade fire, to a distance of about 40 yards from Boynton's front. Its left remained steadfast till Steadman gave way and Boynton withdrew, when the regiment was ordered to the left of Kelly's brigade and joined Triggs in cutting off and capturing several regiments, (See Boynton's report, *supra,* p. 436.) Colonel Palmer estimated the distance of his right from the enemy at 10 or 12 feet. (See Official Records, Series 1, Vol. XXX, Part II, p. 445).

Some Confederate regiment advanced to within 12 or 20 steps of Boynton, because Boynton and Cilley, both saw them from the breastworks, but they could not identify them. Palmer claimed the honor for his regiment, Kelly corroborated his statement, and no one has disputed the claim.

The North Carolina Commission, for whom Colonel Cilley reported, was composed of three soldiers of the 58 N. C., one of whom, Lieut.-Col. I. H. Bailey, a man of high character and who has represented his district creditably, in the State Senate, confirms the statement in his history of the regiment (3 Clark's Regimental Histories, p. 431) as to its proximity to the foe. The other two, Lieut. D. F. Baird and Mr. Davis sustain equally as good reputations. These three men located the Fifty-Eighth, in the charging and fighting line, where Boynton and Cilley saw a Confederate regiment advance and stand. Two distinguished Federal officers determined the position. Three Confederate officers of unquestioned character identify the troops, that occupied the ground. All of the reports place Palmer's regiment on the right of Kelly, and inform us that Gracie gave way, leaving his right exposed, from the very nature of the ground, to an enfilade fire from the line extending east along the Horseshoe, until it was slightly drawn back.

In a letter addressed to the writer of this article dated 15 August, 1904, General Boynton, after expressing his concurrence with General Stewart in the opinion, that the point to which the Sixtieth advanced, is correctly marked by the wooden tablet, says that the Park Commissioners do not know the exact point occupied by the 58 North Carolina, but that the steel tablet erected by the Park Commission indicates the extreme point reached by Kelly's brigade. Gneral Boynton says further,

"My own impression is, indeed it is more than an impression, that whatever regiment occupied the position on the Kelly line of the present tablet, was *certainly no* further than 40 yards to the front of my own regiment, which at that moment held the right of Van Derveer's brigade."

Colonel Kelly, in his report, (Series 1, Vol. XXX, Part II, pp. 438, 439, Official Records), says that the 58th was on his right and that the right of his brigade charged to within 15 or 20, the center 40 and the left 60 yards of the enemy. Kelly gives the formation of his three regiments as follows, the 58th on his right, 5th Kentucky on his left, and the 65th Georgia in the centre.

Colonel Cilley reported, in part, that

"After the fullest discussion, careful examination of printed and verbal testimony, inspection and measurement of ground, *the point where the topmost wave of the tide of Southern battle broke nearer than any other to the unbroken lines*

of Thomas' defense, was agreed by us all to have been reach-
ed by the 58 North Carolina Infantry."

One-half of the soldiers of this untried regiment fell, and
during three hours of continuous fighting, it maintained its
place at the forefront, making only a slight change of part of
its front to conform to the line of the enemy.

Boynton's map of Kelly Field and Snodgrass Hill, on the
afternoon of 20 Sept., (See Chicamauga Military Park,
page 51), shows the position of Preston's division (including
the 58 N. C.), at 4 P. M. and locates it later, at 4:30 P. M.,
as moving up to the position from which Kershaw was driven
back.

We submit that the evidence, from both fighting lines, shows
that the right of Kelly's brigade charged furthest to the front
and that the 58 N. C. was on its right.

It remains only to mention the conduct of the 29 N. C.
Regiment (Infantry) and the 65 N. C. Regiment (6 Cav.)

The Cavalry Regiment, as a part of Davidson's brigade,
Armstrong's Division, Forest's Corps, fought bravely in
advance of our troops on the first day, the 18th, and when
the cavalry encountered, not only Wilder's mounted infantry,
but the brigade of Van Derveer, which won greater distinction than any other troop in Rosecrans' army, the 29 N.
C. met them, and exhibited courage, if not dash, in effect-
ing a crossing of the river.

Unfortunately for the 29 N. C., the report of General Ector,
referred to in Gist's report, was never published, and Colonel
Creasman of that regiment probably made no report of its
conduct at Chickamauga. General Walker said, however:

"General Ector is absent, his brigade having been ordered
to Mississippi, and I have no report from him, but his brigade
acted with the greatest gallantry." (Official Records, Series
1, Vol. XXX, Part II, pp. 240, 246, 247).

Apologizing for its length, I respectfully submit the foregoing, with the hope, that those who may be led by it to search
diligently for the truth, will be fully satisfied, that North
Carolina has claimed for her contingent in the Army of Tennessee no greater distinction than they justly won.

The writer participated in the battle of Chickamauga,
though he has not deemed it proper or necessary to state facts
within his own knowledge, when official documents abundant-

ly establish our contentions. There was but one North Carolina regiment (60 N. C.) in Hill's Corps, of which he was Acting Assistant Inspector General. He placed Cleborne in position on the 19th and again on the 20th before the advance of his Division. He delivered a message to Forest just before the final advance of Hill on the right on Sunday evening, and galloped back to the lines in time to go forward with General Breckenridge to the Chattanooga road, but crossed that road with the Kentucky brigade, not with Stovall's brigade. He did not witness personally the conduct of the 60 N. C., or any other of the North Carolina Regiments. He has recently examined carefully every part of the Park, and satisfied himself of the truth of what he has written. The accompanying map was drawn by W. E. Walton, a civil engineer under his supervision, with aid from the map of Gen. Boynton by his permission and those published in the "Official Records" by U. S. Government.

It is not improper to add, that the writer is under obligation to Captain H. H. Chambers, now a prominent Attorney of the Chattanooga Bar, but a native of North Carolina who won distinction as Captain of Co. C, 49 N. C. Regiment (See 3 "Clark's Regimental Histories," pp. 132, 144), for efficient assistance in the survey of the battle field and in tracing the movements of our regiments.

A. C. AVERY.

MORGANTON, N. C.,
    25 August, 1904.

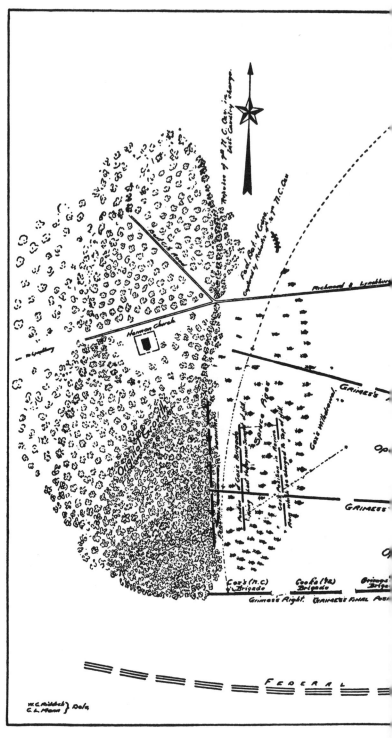

The Last

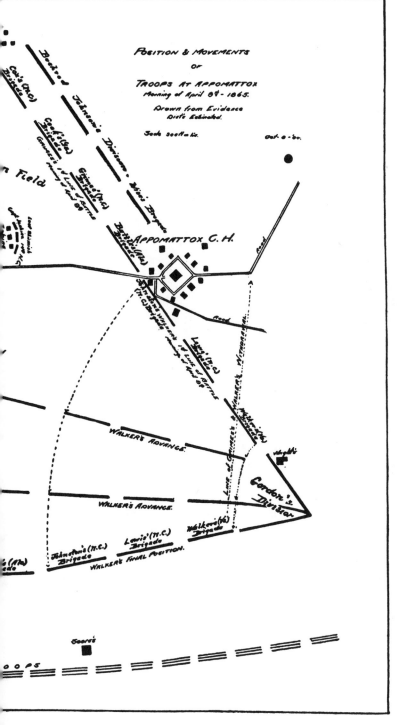

Position & Movements
of
Troops at Appomattox
Morning of April 9 - 1865.
Drawn from Evidence
Dist's Estimated.
Scale 300ft = 1 in.

APPOMATTOX C. H.

WALKER'S ADVANCE.

WALKER'S ADVANCE.

Gordon's
Division

Johnston's (N.C.)
Brigade

Lewis' (N.C.)
Brigade

Walker's (N.C.)
Brigade

WALKER'S FINAL POSITION.

Sears'

ppomattox

Major General Byran Grimes (left) planned and directed the final attack made by the Army of Northern Virginia on April 9, 1865, at Appomattox Court House, Virginia. During the battle, Brigadier General William Ruffin Cox's North Carolina brigade made the last charge and fired the last volley for the Army of Northern Virginia.

Brigadier General William Paul Roberts' (right) brigade, consisting of the 4th and 7th North Carolina Cavalry, captured four artillery pieces (Napoleons) during the morning assault on April 9, 1865, at Appomattox Court House, Virginia. Roberts was the youngest general officer in service for the Confederacy.

"THE LAST AT APPOMATTOX."

By HENRY A. LONDON, Co. I, 32ND N. C. REGIMENT AND COURIER
TO MAJOR-GENERAL BRYAN GRIMES.

North Carolina proudly boasts that she was "The Last at Appomattox" because:

1. A North Carolinian, Major-General Bryan Grimes, planned the last battle fought there and commanded the infantry engaged therein, the greater part of which were North Carolina troops.

2. A North Carolina Brigade, commanded by General W. R. Cox, made the last charge and fired the last volley of any organized body of Confederates immediately preceding the surrender.

3. A detachment of North Carolina troops from the 4th and 14th regiments did the last fighting of any infantry after the withdrawal of the main body of the infantry.

4. North Carolina troops (Roberts' Brigade of cavalry) captured the last cannon that were captured by the Army of Northern Virginia at Appomattox.

In sustaining this proud claim by indisputable proof North Carolina is fortunate in having the full and clear statements written by Major-General Bryan Grimes and Brigadier-General W. R. Cox only a few years after the war, which are as authentic as official reports could be. These statements were published twenty-five years ago and no person has ever denied their entire accuracy and truthfulness. Before they were published they were submitted to this writer for correction or revisal (twenty-five years ago when the incidents of the surrender were fresh in memory) and from personal knowledge I knew them to be true and correct.

The first evidence offered is the statement written by General Grimes in the year 1879 and published in Volume II of Moore's History of North Carolina, from which is copied the following extract:

"On Saturday, the 8th, no enemy appeared, and we marched undisturbed all day. Up to this time, since the evacua-

tion of Petersburg, we had marched day and night, continually followed and harrassed by the enemy. The men were very
much jaded and suffering for necessary sustenance, our halts
not having been sufficiently long to prepare their food, besides
all our cooking utensils not captured or abandoned were where
we could not reach them. This day Bushrod Johnson's Division was assigned to and placed under my command, by order
of General Lee. Upon passing a clear stream of water and
learning that the other divisions of the corps had gone into
camp some two miles ahead, I concluded to halt and give my
broken down men an opportunity to close up and rejoin us,
and sent a message to Major-General John B. Gordon, commanding the Corps, making known my whereabouts, inform-
ing him I would be at any point he might designate at any
hour desired.

"By dark my men were all quiet and asleep. About 9
o'clock I heard the roar of artillery in our front and in consequence of information received, I had my command aroused
in time and passed through the town of Appomattox Court
House before daylight, where, upon the opposite side of the
town, I found the enemy in my front. Throwing out my
skirmishers and forming line of battle, I reconnoitered and
satisfied myself as to their position, and awaited the arrival
of General Gordon for instructions, who, a while before day,
accompanied by General Fitz Lee, came to my position, when
we held a council of war. General Gordon was of the opinion
that the troops in our front were cavalry, and that General
Fitz Lee should attack. Fitz Lee thought they were infantry
and that General Gordon should attack. They discussed the
matter so long that I became impatient, and said it was some-
body's duty to attack, and that immediately, and I felt satisfied that they could be driven from the cross roads occupied
by them, which was the route it was desirable our wagon train
should pursue, and that I would undertake it; whereupon
Gordon said, "Well, drive them off." I replied "I cannot do
it with my division alone, but require assistance." He then
said, "You can take the two other divisions of the Corps."
By this time it was becoming sufficiently light to make the
surrounding localities visible. I then rode down and invited
General Walker, who commanded a division on my left, com-

posed principally of Virginians,* to ride with me, showing him the position of the enemy and explaining to him my views and plan of attack. He agreed with me as to its advisability. I did this because I felt that I had assumed a great responsibility when I took upon myself the charge of making the attack. I then made dispositions to dislodge the Federals from their positions, placing Bushrod Johnson's Division upon my right, with instructions to attack and take the enemy in the flank, while my division skirmishers charged in front, where temporary earthworks had been thrown up by the enemy, their cavalry holding the crossings of the roads with a battery. I soon perceived a disposition on their part to attack this division in flank. I rode back and threw our right so as to take advantage of some ditches and fences to obstruct the cavalry if they should attempt to make a charge. In the mean time the cavalry of Fitz Lee were proceeding by a circuitous route to get in rear of these cross roads. The enemy observing me placing these troops in position, fired upon me with four pieces of artillery. I remember well the appearance of the shell, and how directly they came towards me, exploding and completely enveloping me in smoke. I then gave the signal to advance, at the same time Fitz Lee charged those posted at the cross roads, when my skirmishers attacked the breastworks, which were taken without much loss on my part, also capturing several pieces of artillery and a large number of prisoners, I at the same time moving the division up to the support of the skirmishers in echelon by, brigades, driving the enemy in confusion for three-quarters of a mile beyond the range of hills covered with oak under-

---

* Gen. Grimes was mistaken in saying that the division commanded by Gen. Walker was "composed principally of Virginians". It was composed principally of North Carolinans, one-fourth of that division being Virginians and three-fourths being North Carolinians. This is mentioned by Judge Montgomery on page 260, Vol. V., Clark's Regimental Histories, and is proved by the parole list published on page 1277 of Serial No. 95, of "The Official Records of the Union and Confederate Armies". It will there be seen that Walker's division was composed of Pegram's Virginia brigade with 304 officers and men and R. D. Johnston's North Carolina brigade with 463 and Lewis's North Carolina brigade with 447. So that, in Walker's division there were 910 North Carolinians and 304 Virginians paroled at Appomattox. H. A. L.

growth. I then learned from the prisoners that my right flank was threatened. Halting my troops I placed the skirmishers, commanded by Colonel J. R. Winston, Forty-fifth North Carolina Troops, in front, about one hundred yards distant, to give notice of indications of attack. I placed Cox's Brigade which occupied the right of the division at right angles to the other troops, to watch that flank. The other divisions of the Corps (Walker's and Evans') were on the left. I then sent an officer to General Gordon, announcing our success, and that the Lynchburg road was open for the escape of the wagons, and that I awaited orders. Thereupon I received an order to withdraw, which I declined to do, supposing that General Gordon did not understand the commanding position which my troops occupied. He continued to send me order after order to the same effect, which I still disregarded, being under the impression that he did not comprehend our favorable location, until finally, I received a message from him, with an additional one, as coming from General Lee, to fall back. I felt the difficulty of withdrawing without disaster and ordered Colonel J. R. Winston, commanding the skirmish line which had been posted in my front on first reaching these hills, to conform his movements to those of the division, and to move by the left flank so as to give notice of an attack from that quarter. I then ordered Cox to maintain his position in line of battle, and not to show himself until our rear was one hundred yards distant, and then to fall back in line of battle, so as to protect our rear and right flank from assault. I then instructed Major Peyton, of my staff, to start the left in motion, and I continued with the rear.

"The enemy upon seeing us move off, rushed out from under cover with a cheer, when Cox's brigade, lying concealed at the brow of the hill, rose and fired a volley into them, which drove them back into the woods, the brigade then followed their retreating comrades in line of battle unmolested. After proceeding about half the distance to the position occupied by us in the morning, a dense mass of the enemy in column (infantry), appeared on our right, and advanced, without firing, towards the earthworks captured by us in the early morning, when a battery of our artillery opened with grape and canister and drove them under the shelter of the woods.

"As my troops approached their position of the morning,

I rode up to General Gordon and asked where I should form line of battle. He replied, "Anywhere you choose." Struck by the strangeness of the reply, I asked an explanation, whereupon he informed me that we would be surrendered."

In corroboration of General Grimes is the statement written in 1879 by Brigadier-General William R. Cox and published in Volume II of Moore's History of North Carolina and rewritten without any material change in 1901 and published in Vol. IV of Clark's Regimental Sketches. General Cox's statement is as follows:

"The army now reduced to two corps under Generals Longstreet and Gordon, moved over wretched roads steadily towards Appomattox Court House, our purpose being to reach Danville. By great effort the head of the column reached Appomattox Court House on the evening of the 8th and the troops were halted for rest. During the night there were indications of a large force moving on our left and front. Besides his own division General Grimes was put in command of the remnants of Bushrod Johnson's Division and Wise's Brigade. Just before daylight Gordon moved his command through the village and was supported by Fitz Lee's cavalry on his right. At 5 o'clock a. m. I received an order that on the firing of a cannon the division would move forward. *
* * * * * The division had not proceeded far before Cook's and Cox's Brigades were exposed to a murderous artillery fire, but, instead of halting and recoiling, they promptly charged and captured it. The engagement now became general along our front, and our cavalry, though worn down by incessant duties on the retreat, gallantly and bravely supported us on the right. The struggle, however, was unequal. The pistol and carbine were ineffective against the Enfield range and destructive "buck and ball", and but few infantry were supporting them. Retiring slowly at first their retreat soon became a rout as they hastened to their infantry supports in the woods, while riderless horses galloped over the fields where lay their wounded and dying. An infantry captain was captured and brought before me, and he gave me the first information that General Ord with ten thousand infantry was in our front. Upon taking a commanding position I ordered a halt, when many columns of infantry

were seen advancing, evidently with the intention of capturing us.   Firing was now resumed, when General Grimes
directed me through his courier, H. A. London, to withdraw.
The armistice had evidently been agreed to, but I did not
anticipate it.   Still contesting the field I retired slowly.
The enemy seeing the movement hastened their advance with
the evident purpose of surrounding us and moved so rapidly
as to make some ruse necessary to check their zeal.   In this
emergency, through an aide, James S. Battle, I ordered the
regimental commanders of Cox's Brigade to meet me at the
centre as we retired.   I then directed their attention to a
gradually rising hill between us and the advancing columns of
the enemy, and directed that they face their regiments about
and at a double quick charge to the crest of the hill, and before
the enemy should recover from their surprise, halt, fire by
brigade, and then with like rapid movement face about and
rejoin the division.   Raising the "rebel yell" the brigade with
celerity and precision, promptly and faultlessly executed the
order and having gained the brow of the hill, the enemy an-
ticipating a determined struggle, commenced to deploy and
prolong their line as if on parade.   But before the movement
was fully executed the command rang along the Confederate
line clear and distinct above the din of battle, "Halt, ready,
aim, fire!"   And while the encircling troops were surprised
and stunned by the audacity of the charge and the unusual
character of the fire, the brigade safely withdrew and regain-
ed the division, which in the meantime had been skirmishing
as it withdrew.   General Gordon, superbly mounted, as we
passed by exclaimed, "Grandly and gloriously done!"

"THIS WAS THE LAST CHARGE OF THE ARMY OF
NORTHERN VIRGINIA."

According to the above statements of Generals Grimes and
Cox, written in 1879, and published without any contradic-
tion from any source for more than twenty years, the last
charge made and the last volley fired at Appomattox by any
organized brigade of infantry was by Cox's North Carolina
Brigade.   Their statements are *true of my own personal
knowledge.*
General Cox in his statement further says that "an irregu-

lar exchange of fire was for sometime maintained" by some
of his skirmishers who were covering his retreat and did "not
perceive or understand the flag of truce." In corroboration
of this is the following statement written under date of July
14th, 1904, by Captain W. T. Jenkins, of Halifax county,
who was Captain of Co. A, 14th North Carolina Regiment:

"On the morning of the 9th, after a sleepless and supperless
night, 'very early, while it was yet dark,' we were ordered to
take up line of march in the direction of Lynchburg. We
were marched across a creek beyond Appomattox and formed
line of battle. We were soon ordered to advance down the
Lynchburg road, General Cox's brigade being on the right of
the advancing column. We were discovered by a Yankee
battery on our left and several of our men were killed and
wounded by the shells. We encountered the enemy in force
at an intersection of cross roads and drove them from the field,
and after going some distance on the left of the road we received orders to fall back and bring up the rear. The enemy
soon discovered our retreat and attempted to advance and cut
us off, but we charged and drove them back into the woods and
continued our retreat in the direction of the court-house.
When we reached the road all the troops had passed and we
halted for our rear to come up and all get together.

"General Cox then ordered me to take the 14th and 4th
Regiments and hold the enemy in check until he could get
his command to the rear, and send back some horses and have
a battery of artillery moved which had been left on the road.
I then advanced the two regiments down the road and formed
line of battle, the 4th on the right with left resting on the
road, and the 14th on the left and connecting with the 4th.
We were soon hotly engaged and pressed back, and not wish-
ing to lose all our men and colors I went to the 4th and ordered them to fall back in good order, and then gave the 14th
the same order. I then called for volunteers from the 14th
regiment to take position behind some houses nearby and
hold the enemy in check until the two regiments had gotten
to the rear. About 25 of our men responded promptly and
we soon opened a heavy fire and made a big racket so that
the Yankees did not know our strength.

"While fighting behind those houses two officers rode up

5

some distance in our rear and asked what command was that fighting. We told them "General Cox's." They ordered us to stop firing, saying that General Lee had surrendered. The Yankees were then gathering all around us from right and left, and we saw no way of escape. So, I decided to surrender and hoisted a white flag and went out in front of the houses but we were fired on by the enemy. I suppose they did not see the white flag. Our men opened fire again and kept it up until we were entirely surrounded and taken fighting. Some of our men fired from one corner of a house when the enemy would come around the other. We were taken by Sheridan's command and carried into the Yankee lines and kept all day, and returned to our command about sunset. General Cox and our friends came out to meet us and expressed joy at our return, as they thought we had all been killed. After our surrender or capture we were taken back over the entire battlefield, and I know that there were no other Confederate troops anywhere on the field nor any more firing. . . We were taken I suppose about 12 o'clock. I know the Yankees were eating dinner when we arrived in their camp, and they very kindly offered to share with us but we very politely declined."

The next evidence is that of W. L. London, now the Brigadier General of the second brigade in the North Carolina Division of the United Confederate Veterans, and who was the Adjutant-General of Daniel's (afterwards Grimes') Brigade, and was serving on General Grimes' staff on the morning of the surrender. His written statement under date of August 18, 1904, is as follows:

"On the morning of the ninth of April, 1865, our Brigade being in line of battle, General Grimes rode by and called me to him saying "I want you with me this morning, I have undertaken to open those roads (pointing to the cross-roads in front of us). Your Brigade is so small it will not need you at present." I then rode with him along the lines and just as we were near Wise's Virginia Brigade, the enemy's battery in our front opened on us and one of the shells struck just under General Grimes' horse and so enveloped him in smoke and dust that I thought he must be killed and rode up quickly, but found him unhurt.

"He then told me to ride back and order the line to advance.

When I got to my old regiment (the 32nd) I called their attention to the battery in front and told them I wanted one of those horses, as my horse had given out. It was only a short time before one of the regiment came riding up to the left of the line on a horse from the battery for me, and I brought that horse home with me. I do not know who captured the battery but the 32nd regiment could not have been far off. The line of battle continued to advance and very soon a courier from General Grimes rode up and told General Cox that General Grimes said to fall back, which General Cox soon commenced to do. His men were in a small body of woods, and as soon as his Brigade commenced falling back and had gotten out of the woods, the enemy began to advance in such numbers that it looked like they were rising out of the ground all over the country. General Cox seeing them advancing, ordered his Brigade to 'about-face' and, charging a short distance, fired a volley as one man. This was the last organized firing I heard that day. There were a few sharpshooters protecting the rear and they may have fired some shots. We passed on by the court-house and found all the other troops ahead of us and had halted."

The first troops to reach the battery of artillery, above referred to, were the North Carolina cavalry of General W. P. Roberts, as will be seen from the following letter written to him, under date of July 26, 1904, by his former Adjutant-General, T. S. Garnett, of Norfolk, Virginia:

"My recollection of the capture of a battery of artillery at Appomattox on the morning of the 9th of April, 1865, is simply this: Your Brigade was immediately on the right of Gordon's corps, our left joining Gordon's right and advancing in line with the infantry. The enemy's battery of four Napoleon guns was immediately in our front on open ground, but near a body of woods towards our right. As we advanced the enemy fired repeatedly, their shot being directed chiefly at the infantry of Gordon's corps, and thus affording us an opportunity to get at them easily.

"We approached the battery rapidly and got among them with little loss. They surrendered at once, but one gun limbered up and got away. The captain of the battery surrendered to me and I took his horse from him, telling him to take the captured guns back to Appomattox Court-House and sending Forbes (your courier) back with him. We made their own drivers keep their seats and drive the guns back towards the court-house, where, I afterwards understood, they arrived exactly as ordered. We pressed forward and participated in the continued fighting, passing over a ditch in which I saw the gun which had escaped capture lying overthrown and abandoned. Shortly after this we were ordered to fall back, which we did, returning over the same ground towards the court-house."

In corroboration of the above is the following extract from a written statement, under date of June 2nd, 1904, by Mr. J. P. Leach, of Littleton, who was a member of Co. C, 53rd North Carolina Regiment:

"Our command (Grimes' Division) passed through the town of Appomatox Court House between daybreak and sunrise, when upon the opposite side of the town and within a few hundred yards of the court-house we were put in skirmish line on a road and rail fence. In front of the command and located in a piece of woods, with an open field of several hundred yards between, several pieces of federal artillery had been located and opened fire in the early morning with vigor and unpleasant precision. We were ordered to charge the battery and went forward at double-quick, but before going two hundred yards the guns were silenced and in a few moments were brought galloping toward my command, each gun having six horses. They were turned over to us, and with others I helped to escort the captured battery to a point near the court-house. I trotted along on the off side of a brave and unconcerned "Yank" who rode one of the six bay horses conveying one of the captured guns. He had a haversack hanging on my side of his horse and I an interested witness to its fullness. When we halted near the court-house I proceeded to dislodge from the hames of the horse on my side the food bag of my new acquaintance. He was a stout man and I was a little slender and cadaverous. He raved at me with some cuss words, but I proceeded to open the sack and make fair division with him of our piece of corn beef and six hardtack, the first food I had had for some days. The drivers and artillerymen were very jovial and little concerned about their capture. They could see the game was up with the "Johnnies".

"The battery of four guns had been flanked by cavalry of Gen. Wm. P. Roberts and surrendered to him before the infantry could reach them, a fortunate circumstance which I recall with lasting gratitude for the 'butter-milk' brigade."

With the above evidence of these witnesses, one of them being a Major-General and another being a Brigadier-General, and all except Gen. Grimes still living, North Carolina can safely rest her proud claim of having been "The Last At Appomattox."

HENRY A. LONDON.

PITTSBORO, N. C.,
25 August, 1904.

———

IDENTIFICATION OF LOCALITIES.

The undersigned under instructions of the State Literary and Historical Association visited the battle field at Appomattox Court House on 1 October, 1904, and by personal investigation were enabled to locate the positions described in the foregoing article and to corroborate the statements therein made. Appended hereto is a map of the battlefield and the positions of the North Carolina troops as described in said article, which map is correct and accurate to the personal knowledge of four of the undersigned who were present and participated in the closing scenes at Appomattox.

H. A. LONDON, *32 N. C. Grimes' Brigade,*
W. A. MONTGOMERY, *12 N. C. Johnston's Brigade,*
W. T. JENKINS, *14 N. C. Cox's Brigade,*
A. M. POWELL, *2 N. C. Cox's Brigade,*
W. J. PEELE, *Chmn. N. C. Historical Commission.*

RALEIGH, N C.,
5 October, 1904.

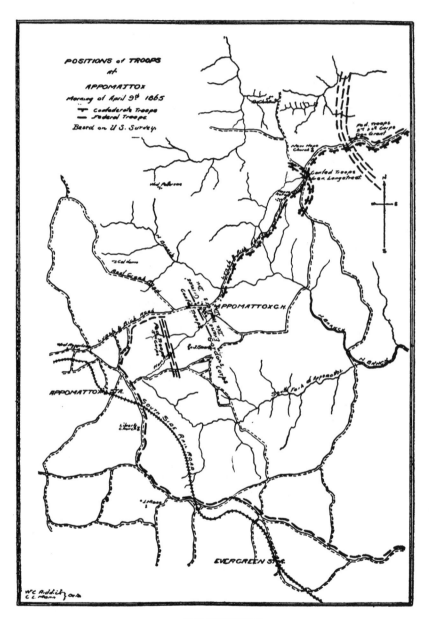

APPOMATTOX

THE LAST CAPTURE OF GUNS.

By E. J. HOLT, 1st LIEUT. 75 N. C., (7 CAV.).

On the night of 8 April, 1865, Roberts' N. C. Cavalry Brigade composed of the 59 and 75 N. C. (4th and 7th cavalry) camped on the Richmond and Lynchburg road, in a piece of woodland about three-fourths or one mile East of Appomattox Court House. About 4 A. M. the morning of the 9th we mounted and were marched through the village to about one-third of a mile West of the Court House and formed in line facing the South-west on the right of Grimes Division next to Cox's N. C. brigade the right of that Division. We remained in that position, mounted, till just about sunrise. The sun came up to our left gloriously bright and warm and cheering to men worn out with cold, hunger, and loss of sleep, as we were. About that time a Chaplain from some regiment in our Division rode out in front of our brigade and made an earnest and fervent prayer. Soon afterwards the enemy began shelling us with a battery a little to the left of our front and about 700 or 800 yards distant. The battery was in an open field and near to woodland on its left and rear, and was on very much lower land than the position held by us. Promptly General W. P. Roberts' Brigade, composed of what was left of the 59 N. C. (4th Cav.) and the 75 N. C. (7th Cav.)—in all, I suppose, near 100 men—charged, in line, with drawn sabres directly upon the battery, which was supported by a force of Sheridan's dismounted cavalry. Our charge was first met by shells, then grape, and then by canister and the balls from the carbines. We moved very rapidly, and, the surface of the land being undulating, we were frequently out of sight of the battery and safe from their grape. When we got within about 200 yards of them they began to run. Some went into the woods, some took shelter under the gun carriages, and all quit firing. Our loss was very light. We captured four Napoleons and about fifty men.

As quickly as possible we took our guns and prisoners back to the point where we had first formed our line that morning, and proceeded at once to re-form our commands and get ready for other work.   About the time we got in order again, one of the men in the 75th called my attention to a small force of the enemy going South-easterly down a rail fence between the woods and fields, at a point marked "C" on the map.   I called to General Roberts and pointed them out, and after a hasty examination with his field glass, he ordered the 75th to charge and capture them.   We at once drew sabres and charged in columns of four.   The field was intersected by ditches and my idea was to charge in columns of fours and, when we had passed the last ditch, to deploy into line and then give them the sabre.   But when we had crossed, as I thought, the last ditch and begun our movement to get into line, I discovered a large ditch just inside the field and saw at once that our horses could not get over the ditch and the rail fence built upon the earth taken from the ditch.   Our Yankees quit going down the fence and dropped on their knees and opened on us with a hot fire with Spencer rifles.   I saw that it was impossible to reach them with the sabre and gave the order to unsling carbines and fire.   We gave them a volley, and about that time my horse was killed; and seeing the utter uselessness of our staying there to be butchered, with no hope of getting at our enemy.   I gave orders to fall back.   I went out on foot and was exposed to a warm fire for the first two hundred yards.   Two balls cut my clothing.   I ran in a North-easterly direction and got to the Richmond and Lynchburg road, about 200 yards from the Court House.   While falling back I noticed there was no firing, either by cannon or small arms, and just before I got to the road I saw a party with a flag of truce going towards the Court House.   I suppose it was about 9 A. M. And from what I know to have been done that eventful morning, I feel sure that the 75th N. C. (7th Cav.) was up against the enemy about as late as Cox's N. C. Infantry Brigade to our left and entitled to share in the honor of having fought as long as any other troops.   Certainly it is beyond question that we captured four cannon and about fifty men, the last capture that was made by that immortal army that had captured so many men and guns in its history.

E. J. HOLT.

SMITHFIELD, N. C.,
        7 October, 1904.

NUMBER AND LOSSES OF NORTH CAROLINA TROOPS.

By CAPT. S. A. ASHE.

Although North Carolina had not been favorable to Secession at an early stage of the troubles between the North and South, yet when the fight came on, her contributions to the Southern Cause were more important than those of any other State. Alone of all her sister States, she made importations of supplies from abroad that were of great consequence. During the Revolutionary War, she had employed a Board of Officers to collect and export produce and to import necessaries and munitions; and in 1861, history repeated itself, and she early made a large appropriation to purchase supplies abroad, and later under Gov. Vance's administration, she bought a fast vessel and imported large quantites of mill supplies, 60,000 pairs of hand cards, 10,000 grain scythes, shoes and leather for shoes equal to 250,000 pairs, 50,000 blankets, grey woolen cloth for 250,000 uniforms, 12,000 overcoats, $50,000 gold value of medicines and many other supplies. As the shoes, blankets and clothing were more than sufficient for the use of her own troops, large quantites of them were turned over to the Confederate Government for the troops of other States. The wisdom of the North Carolina statesmen made them provident for the supply of the Army; and in like manner, their spirit and zeal led them to cooperate with the Confederate Government in the enforcement of the conscript act to an extent beyond what obtained elsewhere. In no other State was the conscript act enforced so thoroughly as in North Carolina, the State authorities aiding in its enforcement.

The contribution of the State in soldiers was indeed remarkable, and in losses she suffered much more than any other State.

Major-General R. C. Gatlin, who had been a distinguished officer of the U. S. Army, while Adjutant General of the State of North Carolina, on May 16, 1864, reported "that

"up to the 31st of March, 1864, North Carolina had furnish-"
"ed troops as follows:

"Transferred to the Confederate States according to
    the original rolls (August 20, 1862),..........   64,436
Estimated number of recruits that have volunteered
    in the different companies' service, since the date
    of the original rolls.......................   20,608
Number of conscripts sent to the army..........   14,460
Number of troops in the service of the State not
    transferred, ...   2,903

Making an aggregate of...................... 102,607
    These troops have been organized as follows:
Regiments of Artillery.........................   3
Regiments of Cavalry..........................   6
Regiments of Infantry.........................   60

Total number of Regiments.....................   69
Battalions of Artillery..........................   4
Battalions of Cavalry..........................   4
Battalions of Infantry.........................   3

Total number of Battalions.....................   11
    Unattached Companies, infantry................   6"

"There is one Company from this State in the 10th Virginia Cavalry, five in the 7th Confederate Cavalry, four in the 62nd Georgia Regiment, and one in the 61st Virginia Infantry." That was March, 1864,

On July 7, 1863, the General Assembly of North Carolina passed an Act to organize the Guard for Home Defence, to be composed of all persons between the ages of 18 and 50, not actually in the service of the Confederate States. These were enrolled and organized into companies, and regiments, and those across the Blue Ridge into a Brigade and John W. McElroy was appointed a Brigadier-General, and assigned to the command with head quarters at Burnsville.

The number of Home Guard enrolled was 28,098; but a large number of them were cripples, infirm and decrepit, and unfit to perform military duty. Boards of Examiners were appointed to pass on all claims of exemption on account of physical disability; but before that work was completed, the Confederate law putting all persons between the ages of 17 and 50 into the Confederate service was passed and that largely reduced the Home Guard organizations. But the Home Guard under General McElroy was early called out and was in active service; and the Home Guard of the Eastern Counties were later organized into a brigade under General Collett Leventhorpe, and the Home Guard of other counties were also in active service.

Governor Vance in his address at White Sulphur Springs in 1875 after a careful examination of the records of the Adjutant General's office, stated the North Carolina troops in the war as follows:

"Volunteers at the outset...................... 64,636
Volunteers subsequently received............... 21,608
Troops in unattached companies in Regiments of
    other States 3,103
Regular troops in States's service.............. 3,203
Conscripts sent to the front.................. 18,585
Senior Reserves 5,686
Junior Reserves 4,217
                                             ————
Home Guard 3,962
                                             ————
                                            125,000"

And these figures are as correct as it is possible to make them.

The Senior and Junior Reserves were organized into Regiments and were trained troops and were incorporated into the Army and were therefore to be numbered with the Regular forces of the Confederacy.

The figures for the Confederate Army, now accepted, were estimated by Dr. Joseph Jones and were approved by General Cooper, the Adjutant General of the Confederacy. (See p. 287, 7th Vol., Southern Historical Society papers). "The available Confederate force capable of active service in the field did not during the entire war exceed 600,000 men; and of this number not more than 400,000 were enrolled at any one time."

However, at page 500, Vol. 12, Confederate Military History, the total number borne on the Confederate Muster Roll on January 1st, 1864, is stated at 472,781; but these figures include the absent as well as the present, the prisoners in Northern prisons and the sick at home as well as all absent without leave. Indeed it is estimated that not more than 200,000 Confederate soldiers ever were present in the Camps and ready for battle at any one time.

The entire Military population of the eleven seceded States was 1,064,193; and that of North Carolina was 115,369, being one ninth of the whole.

Military population embraces all white males between the ages of 18 and 45 without regard to any physical or mental infirmity or religious scruples; and making some allowance for these exemptions, the Military population of North Carolina would be diminshed by several thousand.

Taking the entire enrollment of Confederate Troops at 600,000 and North Carolina's contribution at 125,000, it appears that she furnished something more than one fifth of all the soldiers who were enrolled beneath the flag of the Confederacy, although her military population was only one ninth of the whole.

Of those present for duty, it would seem that North Carolina had a much larger proportion than would have naturally fallen to her lot. It was the policy founded in wisdom to keep her regiments full and effective and not to multiply her organizations. We find that the enrollment of some of her regiments aggregated 1800; as some were killed or died, new men replaced them and the organizations were thus maintained effective until towards the very end of the war.

There were altogether 529 Regiments and 85 Battalions of infantry in the Confederate service, and enough of the other branches of the service to make the entire force equivalent to 764 regiments of 10 companies each. (Colonel Fox's Regimental Losses, page 553). Of these organizations, Virginia had somewhat more than one tenth and North Carolina somewhat less than one tenth. How full North Carolina kept her regiments relatively is demonstrated by the fact that with less than one tenth of the organizations, she furnished one fifth of the soldiers. It is apparent that relatively her organizations were kept fuller than those of other States.

And the same conclusion must be reached when we consider the losses in battle. The valor of the Confederate troops from the different States was much the same. The fortunes of the battlefield brought heavy losses to regiments from every State without much discrimination. Evidently then, losses on the battlefield measurably indicate the numbers engaged from the different States.

Of the Confederate losses on the battlefield and died from wounds, North Carolina's proportion was more than 25 per cent. The entire Confederate loss was 74,524, and that of North Carolina was 19,673, which was more than one fourth. (Fox's Regimental Losses, page 554). It would seem therefore that on the basis of losses, one fourth of all the troops engaged in the battles of the war, were from North Carolina.

Now turning to the statistics in regard to deaths by disease, 59,297 are reported to have died of disease, of whom 20,602 were North Carolinians. (Fox's Regimental Losses, p. 554). As her troops were no more liable to disease than those from other States, and perhaps not so much so since they were better cared for, it would seem from this that her enrollment approximated one third of the entire enrollment of the Confederate Army. These indications irresistibly lead to the conclusion that North Carolina was constantly represented in the field by a much larger number of soldiers present for duty than any other State.

The white population of Virginia was 1,047,299 and her military population was 196,587. The entire population, black and white, of that part of Virginia subsequently cut off was about 400,000, leaving the State of Virginia with a larger white population and a larger military population than North Carolina.

The white enlistments in the Federal Army for North Carolina were 3,146; and the white enlistments in the Federal Army from West Virginia were 31,872.

If four tenths of Virginia's white population should be assigned to West Virginia, and six tenths to the State of Virginia, her military population being six tenths of the entire military population according to the census, would be about 120,000.

While that is larger than the military population of North Carolina, yet the military strength of these States was so nearly equal that a comparison can justly be made between them to illustrate how fully and nobly North Carolina performed her duty to the Confederacy.

The losses attributed to Virginia (See Fox's Regimental Losses, p. 554) were killed outright on the battlefield, 5,328, and died of wounds, 2,519, a total of 7,847. There is no reason why Virginia's losses suffered on the battlefield should not have been as accurately reported as those of North Carolina. North Carolina's losses are reported at 19,673; Virginia's at 7,847, from which it appears that North Carolina lost on the battlefield more than twice as many soldiers as Virginia did.

The same authority states that Virginia lost 6,947 from disease, and North Carolina lost 20,602, nearly three times as many.

The inference is irresistible, that North Carolina contributed more men to the Confederate service than Virginia did.

At page 553, Fox states that North Carolina had 69 regiments and 4 battalions of infantry; one regiment and five battalions of cavalry and 2 battalions of heavy artillery and 9 battalions of light artillery. As a matter of fact it appears that North Carolina furnished 84 regiments, 16 battalions, and 13 unattached Companies, besides the companies and individuals serving in commands from other States, and 9 regiments of Home Guards, and the militia rendering short terms of duty. Vol. 4, p. 224, Reg. Histories. Virginia is credited with 65 regiments and 10 battalions of infantry, 22 regiments and 11 battalions of cavalry, one regiment of partizan rangers, one regiment of artillery and 53 batteries of light artillery. But how many of these organizations were maintained with their full complement of men ready for active duty does not appear. It does appear however that North Carolina furnished more than 120,000 soldiers including Home Guard out of a total enrollment of 600,000, leaving only 480,000 to be apportioned among the other States. It also appears that her losses both on the battlefield and by disease indicate that her contribution to the Confederate Army was somewhat more than the proportion of one to five, while her military population stood in proportion of one to nine.

This record is one that every Confederate in North Carolina can recall with the utmost pride and satisfaction. It sustains the claim made in behalf of our people that they sent to the war for Southern Independence a greater number of soldiers in proportion to population than any other Southern State, and that they suffered the heaviest losses.

S. A. Ashe.

Raleigh N. C.,
25 August, 1904.

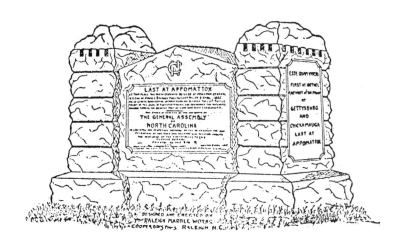

The North Carolina Monument at Appomattox.

THE MONUMENT

Inscriptions on Monument

LAST AT APPOMATTOX. At this place the North Carolina Brigade of Brigadier-General W. R. Cox, of Grimes's Division fired the last volley 9 April 1865. Major General Byran Grimes of North Carolina planned the last battle fought by the Army of Northern Virginia and commanded the infantry engaged therein, the greater part of whom were North Carolinians.

This stone is erected by the authority of the General Assembly of North Carolina in grateful and perpetual memory of the valor, endurance and patriotism of her sons who followed with unshaken fidelity the fortunes of the Confederacy to this closing scene. Faithful to the end.

Erected 9 April 1905. North Carolina Appomattox Commission: H. A. London, Chairman: W. T. Jenkins, E. J. Holt, Cyrus B. Watson, A. D. McGill.

North Carolina troops paroled at Appomattox. Brigades. Cox's 572, Grimes' 530, Johnston's 63, Lewis' 447, Cooke's 560, MacRae's 442, Lane's 570, Scales' 719, Ransom's 435, Barringer's 23, Roberts' 93. Major-General Grimes and Staff 8. Cumming's, Miller's, Williams', Flanner's and Ramsay's Batteries 150. Total North Carolina Paroled 5,012.

Esse Quam Videri. First at Bethel. Farthest to the front at Gettysburg and Chickamauga. Last at Appomattox.

North Carolina, 1860 White population 629, 942; Military population 115,369. 1861-1865 Troops furnished 127,000; Killed in battle 14,522; Died from wounds 5,151; Died from disease 20,602.

The other two monuments bear the following inscriptions: North Carolina. At this place was fought the last skirmish by Captain Wilson T. Jenkins of the Fourteenth North Carolina Regiment, commanding twenty-five men of the Fourth and Fourteenth North Carolina Regiments.

North Carolina. The last Federal battery taken by the Confederates was captured by the North Carolina Cavalry Brigade of Brig-Gen. W. P. Roberts at this place.

Sergeant Murdock H. Smith
2nd North Carolina Artillery
(United States Army Military History Institute Collection)

Captain J. M. Hadley
Assistant Surgeon
4th North Carolina Infantry
(North Carolina State Archives Collection)
(See pages 59 and 65 for the exploits of the 4th at Appomattox)

Private John Wesley Knott
Company A, 6th North Carolina Infantry
(Richard Zigler Collection at USAMHI)

Captain Jacob Allison Fisher
9th North Carolina Infantry and 16th North Carolina Cavalry
(Alex Campbell Collection at USAMHI)

Captain Egbert A. Ross
11th North Carolina Infantry
(Douglas Moore Collection at USAMHI)
(See page 36 about the 11th at Gettysburg)

Private John Wesley Duckett
Company C, 29th North Carolina Infantry
(Mable Duckett Collection at USAMHI)
(See pages 47 and 56 for the role of the 29th at Chickamauga)

Second Lieutenant Stephen Harrison Miller
Company F, 29th North Carolina Infantry
(Sally A. Warren Collection at USAMHI)
(See pages 47 and 56 regarding the 29th at Chickamauga)

Private Elisha E. House
Company C, 38th North Carolina Infantry
(North Carolina State Archives Collection)
(See pages 36 and 44 concerning the 38th at Gettysburg)

Sergeant Ransom M. Middleton
Company A, 38th North Carolina Infantry
(Frank Middleton Collection at USAMHI)
(See page 36 and 44 about the 38th at Gettysburg)

Sergeant Peter Jones
Company I, 45th North Carolina Infantry
(North Carolina State Archives Collection)
(See page 62 to read about the 45th at Appomattox)

First Lieutenant and Adjutant William H. Young
55th North Carolina Infantry
(USAMHI Collection)
(See pages 36 and 44 regarding the 55th at Gettysburg)

For a complete book and price list write:

Schroeder Publications
12 Camellia Drive
Daleville, VA 24083
www.civilwar-books.com
Email: paspub@rbnet.com

Other Titles Available:

* **Thirty Myths About Lee's Surrender** by Patrick A. Schroeder
  ISBN 1-889246-05-0

* **More Myths About Lee's Surrender** by Patrick A. Schroeder
  ISBN 1-889246-01-8

* **The Confederate Cemetery at Appomattox** by Patrick A. Schroeder
  ISBN 1-889246-11-5

* **Recollections & Reminiscences of Old Appomattox and Its People**
  by George T. Peers ISBN 1-889246-12-3

* **The Fighting Quakers** by A. J. H. Duganne ISBN 1-889246-03-4

* **A Duryée Zouave** by Thomas P. Southwick ISBN 1-889246-24-7

* **Civil War Soldier Life: In Camp and Battle** by George F. Williams
  ISBN 1-889246-04-2

* **We Came To Fight: The History of the 5th New York Veteran Volunteer
  Infantry, Duryee's Zouaves, (1863-1865)** by Patrick A. Schroeder
  ISBN 1-889246-07-7

* **A Swedish Officer in the American Civil War: The Diary of Axel Leatz of
  the 5th New York Veteran Volunteer Infantry, Duryée's Zouaves,
  (1863-1865)** edited by Patrick Schroeder ISBN 1-889246-06-9

* **Campaigns of the 146th Regiment New York State Volunteers**
  by Mary Genevie Green Brainard ISBN 1-889246-08-5

* **The Bloody 85th: The Letters of Milton McJunkin, A Western
  Pennsylvania Soldier in the Civil War** edited by Richard Sauers, Ronn
  Palm, and Patrick A. Schroeder ISBN 1-889246-13-1

* **The Pennsylvania Bucktails: A Photographic Album of the 42nd, 149th &
  150th Pennsylvania Regiments** by Patrick A. Schroeder and Ronn Palm
  ISBN 1-889246-14-X